WITHDRAWN FROM TSC LIBRARY

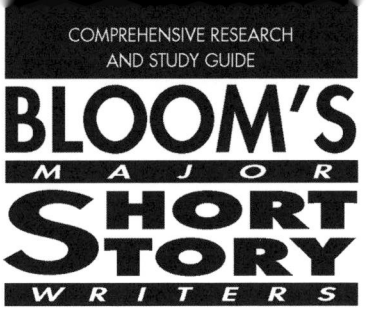

BLOOM'S MAJOR SHORT STORY WRITERS

Jorge Luis **Borges**

EDITED AND WITH AN INTRODUCTION BY HAROLD BLOOM

CURRENTLY AVAILABLE

BLOOM'S MAJOR DRAMATISTS

Aeschylus
Aristophanes
Bertold Brecht
Anton Chekhov
Henrik Ibsen
Ben Johnson
Christopher Marlowe
Arthur Miller
Eugene O'Neill
Shakespeare's Comedies
Shakespeare's Histories
Shakespeare's Romances
Shakespeare's Tragedies
George Bernard Shaw
Neil Simon
Oscar Wilde
Tennessee Williams
August Wilson

BLOOM'S MAJOR NOVELISTS

Jane Austen
The Brontës
Willa Cather
Stephen Crane
Charles Dickens
William Faulkner
F. Scott Fitzgerald
Nathaniel Hawthorne
Ernest Hemingway
Henry James
James Joyce
D. H. Lawrence
Toni Morrison
John Steinbeck
Stendhal
Leo Tolstoy
Mark Twain
Alice Walker
Edith Wharton
Virginia Woolf

BLOOM'S MAJOR POETS

Maya Angelou
Elizabeth Bishop
William Blake
Gwendolyn Brooks
Robert Browning
Geoffrey Chaucer
Sameul Taylor Coleridge
Dante
Emily Dickinson
John Donne
H.D.
T. S. Eliot
Robert Frost
Seamus Heaney
Homer
Langston Hughes
John Keats
John Milton
Sylvia Plath
Edgar Allan Poe
Poets of World War I
Shakespeare's Poems & Sonnets
Percy Shelley
Alfred, Lord Tennyson
Walt Whitman
William Carlos Williams
William Wordsworth
William Butler Yeats

BLOOM'S MAJOR SHORT STORY WRITERS

Jorge Louis Borges
Italo Calvino
Raymond Carver
Anton Chekhov
Joseph Conrad
Stephen Crane
William Faulkner
F. Scott Fitzgerald
Nathaniel Hawthorne
Ernest Hemingway
O. Henry
Shirley Jackson
Henry James
James Joyce
Franz Kafka
D.H. Lawrence
Jack London
Thomas Mann
Herman Melville
Flannery O'Connor
Edgar Allan Poe
Katherine Anne Porter
J. D. Salinger
John Steinbeck
Mark Twain
John Updike
Eudora Welty

COMPREHENSIVE RESEARCH
AND STUDY GUIDE

Jorge Luis
Borges

EDITED AND WITH AN INTRODUCTION BY HAROLD BLOOM

© 2002 by Chelsea House Publishers, a subsidiary of
Haights Cross Communications.

Introduction © 2002 by Harold Bloom.

All rights reserved. No part of this publication may be reproduced
or transmitted in any form or by any means without the written
permission of the publisher.

Printed and bound in the United States of America.

First Printing
1 3 5 7 9 8 6 4 2

Library of Congress Cataloging-in-Publication Data

Jorge Luis Borges / Harold Bloom, ed.
    p. cm. — (Bloom's major short story writers)
   Includes bibliographical references and index.
   ISBN 0-7910-6823-4
   1. Borges, Jorge Luis, 1899—Criticism and interpretation. I.
Bloom,
Harold. II. Series.
PQ7797.B635 Z745 2002
868'.6209—dc21
                                    2002002775

Chelsea House Publishers
1974 Sproul Road, Suite 400
Broomall, PA 19008-0914

The Chelsea House World Wide Web address is http://www.chelseahouse.com

Contributing Editor: Elizabeth Beaudin

Layout by EJB Publishing Services

CONTENTS

User's Guide	7
About the Editor	8
Editor's Note	9
Introduction	10
Biography of Jorge Luis Borges	12
Plot Summary of "Death and the Compass"	16
List of Characters in "Death and the Compass"	21
Critical Views on "Death and the Compass"	23
Jorge Luis Borges on the story	23
Edna Aizenberg on Jewish Elements and Spinoza	24
Harold Bloom on Aesthetic Motivations	28
Carlos Fuentes on City and Fiction	29
Jorge Hernández Martín on Detective Fiction	31
Svend Østergård on Representation	33
Floyd Merrell on Labyrinths and the Story	35
Plot Summary of "Tlön, Uqbar, Orbis Tertius"	40
List of Characters in "Tlön, Uqbar, Orbis Tertius"	45
Critical Views on "Tlön, Uqbar, Orbis Tertius"	47
Didier T. Jaén on Esoteric Tradition	47
Evelyn Fishburn and Psiche Hughes: Definition of Orbus Tertius	49
Roberto González Echevarría on the Story	50
Beatriz Urraca on Mirrors and Tlön	53
Sylvia Molloy on Language	55
Gabriel Josipovici on Ideologies	57
Jorge Luis Borges Interview on Tlön	60
Plot Summary of "The Immortal"	62
List of Characters in "The Immortal"	66
Critical Views on "The Immortal"	67
George R. McMurray on an Allegory of the Creative Process	67
Michael Evans on Intertextuality	68
Evelyn Fishburn and Psiche Hughes: Definition of Joseph Cartaphilus	70
Evelyn Fishburn and Psiche Hughes: Definition of Argos	70

Jon Stewart on Christian View of Immortality	71
Harold Bloom on the Irony Present in the Story	73
Dominique Jullien on Biographies of an Immortal	74
René de Costa on Humor in Borges	76
Plot Summary of "The Aleph"	79
List of Characters in "The Aleph"	82
Critical Views on "The Aleph"	84
Jorge Luis Borges Writing About "The Aleph"	84
Jon Thiem on Borges-Dante Parallels	85
Evelyn Fishburn and Psiche Hughes: Definition of Aleph	86
María Rosa Menocal on Visions of Beatriz/Beatrice	87
Jorge Luis Borges on the Story	90
Nada Elia on Islamic Mysticism in the Story	91
María Kodama on Mystical Experience	93
Plot Summary of "The South"	96
List of Characters in "The South"	99
Critical Views on "The South"	100
Jorge Luis Borges on the Story	100
Jaime Alazraki on Structure and Autobiography in the Story	101
Ana María Barrenchea on Repetition in Texts	104
Evelyn Fishburn and Psiche Hughes: Definition of Gaucho	105
Didier T. Jaén on Time (Fiction/Loss) in the Story	106
Jorge Luis Borges on the Story	108
Works by Jorge Luis Borges	110
Principal Translations in English	112
Works about Jorge Luis Borges	113
Acknowledgments	117
Index of Themes and Ideas	120

USER'S GUIDE

This volume is designed to present biographical, critical, and bibliographical information on the author and the author's best-known or most important short stories. Following Harold Bloom's editor's note and introduction is a concise biography of the author that discusses major life events and important literary accomplishments. A plot summary of each story follows, tracing significant themes, patterns, and motifs in the work. An annotated list of characters supplies brief information on the main characters in each story. As with any study guide, it is recommended that the reader read the story beforehand, and have a copy of the story being discussed available for quick reference.

A selection of critical extracts, derived from previously published material, follows each character list. In most cases, these extracts represent the best analysis available from a number of leading critics. Because these extracts are derived from previously published material, they will include the original notations and references when available. Each extract is cited, and readers are encouraged to check the original publication as they continue their research. A bibliography of the author's writings, a list of additional books and articles on the author and their work, and an index of themes and ideas conclude the volume.

ABOUT THE EDITOR

Harold Bloom is Sterling Professor of the Humanities at Yale University and Henry W. and Albert A. Berg Professor of English at the New York University Graduate School. He is the author of over 20 books, and the editor of more than 30 anthologies of literary criticism.

Professor Bloom's works include *Shelly's Mythmaking* (1959), *The Visionary Company* (1961), *Blake's Apocalypse* (1963), *Yeats* (1970), *A Map of Misreading* (1975), *Kabbalah and Criticism* (1975), *Agon: Toward a Theory of Revisionism* (1982), *The American Religion* (1992), *The Western Canon* (1994), and *Omens of Millennium: The Gnosis of Angels, Dreams, and Resurrection* (1996). *The Anxiety of Influence* (1973) sets forth Professor Bloom's provocative theory of the literary relationships between the great writers and their predecessors. His most recent books include *Shakespeare: The Invention of the Human*, a 1998 National Book Award finalist, *How to Read and Why* (2000), and *Stories and Poems for Extremely Intelligent Children of All Ages* (2001).

Professor Bloom earned his Ph.D. from Yale University in 1955 and has served on the Yale faculty since then. He is a 1985 MacArthur Foundation Award recipient and served as the Charles Eliot Norton Professor of Poetry at Harvard University in 1987–88. In 1999 he was awarded the prestigious American Academy of Arts and Letters Gold Medal for Criticism. Professor Bloom is the editor of several other Chelsea House series in literary criticism, including BLOOM'S MAJOR SHORT STORY WRITERS, BLOOM'S MAJOR NOVELISTS, BLOOM'S MAJOR DRAMATISTS, MODERN CRITICAL INTERPRETATIONS, MODERN CRITICAL VIEWS, and BLOOM'S BIOCRITIQUES.

EDITOR'S NOTE

My Introduction comments upon all five of the stories studied in this volume, and seeks to emphasize those qualities that must render them Borgesian.

On "Death and the Compass," Borges himself sets the background, after which Edna Aizenberg examines the Jewish aspects of the story. I brood on Borgesian aesthetic ethos, while the Mexican novelist Carlos Fuentes returns us to Borges's visionary Buenos Aires, and Jorge Hernández Martín invokes the literary context of detective fiction. The story's shifting perspectives are analyzed by Svend Østergård, and then Floyd Merrell explores the symbol of the labyrinth.

"Tlön, Uqbar, Orbis Tertius" is located in esoteric tradition by Didier Jaén, while Roberto González Echevarría relates the story to ethnographic technique. In turn, mirrors, philosophic systems, and ideologies are considered, respectively, by Beatriz Urraca, Sylvia Molloy, and Gabriel Josipovici.

With "The Immortal," we are given George McMurray on allegory, Michael Evans on intertextuality, Jon Stewart on Christian parody, while I, Dominique Jullien, and René de Costa in different ways examine the story's ironies.

"The Aleph" is seen in relation to Dante by Jon Thiem and María Rosa Menocal, after which Nada Elia and María Kodama comment on mysticism in the story.

Borges himself sets forth three ways of reading. "The South," while Jaime Alazraki, Ana María Barrenchea, and Didier T. Jaén define problems in its structure.

INTRODUCTION
Harold Bloom

This little volume presents critical views of wide range and considerable utility on five remarkable stories by the great Argentine fabulist, Jorge Luis Borges.

"Death and the Compass," a personal favorite, displays Borges both as ironist and as Kabbalist, two of his crucial aesthetic stances. The antagonists, the detective Erik Lönnrot and the Jewish gangster, Dandy Red Scharlach, essentially are the same person. Though Scharlach entraps Lönnrot in a speculative labyrinth, and then murders him, the aesthetic triumph belongs to the suicidal quester Lönnrot, who offers a critique of Scharlach's plot that Scharlach accepts. Borges's "Death and the Compass" is a distinguished culmination of the Western literary theme of the Double, previously explored by Hoffmann, Poe, Dostoevsky and Conrad, among so many others.

The fantasy, "Tlön, Uqbar, Orbis Tertius," carries the Borgesian ironic esotericism to a sublime limit of ambivalence. Aesthetically, Borges is fascinated by imagined lands, since they are the ultimate instances of Platonism or Idealism. The Gnostic "Third World" or Imaginal Realm (as Henry Corbin termed it) appeals to what is most profound in Borges's own consciousness. And yet he was very wary of the ideologies that pragmatically manifested such tendencies: Marxism, Fascism, and all their variants. There is a perilous balance in Borgesian fantasy, which cautions us against the degeneration of vision into ideologies and political hellishness.

Borges's more strictly literary irony triumphs in "The Immortal," in which Swiftian satire, George Bernard Shaw's Creative Evolution in Back to Methuselah, and the dream visions of Thomas DeQuincy are fused into a parodistic nightmare that destroys both the Christian myth of immortality and the literary contest for canonical survival. Most powerfully, Borges turns against his own literary idealism, in which the identities of Homer, Shakespeare, and Borges merge into one another. A kind of horror, juxtaposed with fierce comedy, makes "The Immortal" a unique triumph of contraries, even for Borges.

The mysterious splendor of "The Aleph" again unites Kabbalah and Islamic esotericism with subtle Borgesian irony. The Aleph in one sense is a Kabbalistic and Sufi talisman, a microcosm that contains all multiplicity in a single, small icon. Daneri's poem (surely Borges was satirizing Pablo Neruda's Canto general) is a poor rival for the Aleph, and by ultimate implication, even Dante's Commedia must compare weakly to the Aleph, despite Dante's enormous imaginative achievement in a structured vision.

With "The South," Borges takes us to a border between dream and realistic representation. Dahlmann faces imminent death, or a dream of it. What matters aesthetically is the astonishing vividness and rightness of the story. Dahlmann is the emblem of Borges's own aesthetic dignity, of the writer's love of autonomy and of legitimate pride.

BIOGRAPHY OF
Jorge Luis Borges

On August 24, 1899, Jorge Luis Borges, the creator of memorable labyrinths and fantasies, was born in Buenos Aires, Argentina, to Guillermo Borges, a lawyer and psychology teacher, and Leonor Acevedo Suárez, who would be a formidable presence in her son's life. His beloved sister Norah was born in 1902. His family heritage was diverse and rich. Men on both sides of his family had fought for independence in Argentina. Jorge Luis inherited from his father his poor eyesight as well as his English and Portuguese background; his mother provided his ties to Uruguay. His father also encouraged his son to study and use the family library such that at the age of seven, Jorge Luis was able to write a composition in English on Greek mythology and a story in Spanish entitled "La visera fatal" based on an idea in Cervantes's *Don Quixote*. Continuing in this precocious vein, during his childhood Borges translated Oscar Wilde's *The Happy Prince* into Spanish and published his first short story called "King of the Jungle."

Shortly before the start of World War I in 1914, the senior Borges's failing sight forced his retirement. The Borges family moved to Europe where they visited London, Paris, and northern Italy before arriving in Geneva where they spent the next four years. During this time, Borges already fluent in Spanish and English, began his studies of French and Latin. Borges also taught himself German. His reading material during this period was robust and included Victor Hugo in French, Nietzsche and Schopenhauer in German, and Carlyle and Chesterton in English. It was during this time that he discovered the work of Walt Whitman.

After the war, the family moved to Spain, and in 1919, Borges came under the influence of Rafael Cansinos-Assens and several Ultraist poets in Madrid. He focused his studies on Spanish literature and published his first poem "Hymn to the Sea" in *Grecia*. In 1919, the Borges family returned to Buenos Aires, and in 1921 Borges began the avant-garde review, *Prisma*, which lasted two issues. During this period, Macedonio Fernández, a family friend and cofounder of the magazine *Proa*, mentored Jorge Luis, and in 1923,

Borges published his first book of poetry, *Fervor de Buenos Aires (Passion for Buenos Aires)*.

His literary life progressed over the next several years with, in 1925, Borges publishing a second book of poems, *Luna de Enfrente (Moon Across the Way)* in 1925, and *Inquisiciones (Inquisitions)*, his first book of essays. In 1930, he began a lifelong friendship and literary collaboration with fellow Argentine, Adolfo Bioy Casares (*Invención de Morel*, 1940). Borges also contributed often to the fundamental Argentine literary journal of the day, *Sur*, founded by friend and colleague, Victoria Ocampo. In 1933, Borges became the literary editor of the Saturday supplement for *Crítica*. Two years later, his first book of stories, *Historia universal de la infamia (A Universal History of Infamy)*, was released and it contained several pieces published earlier in *Crítica*.

Both his father's health and Borges's own health colored the next few years of his life. Because of his father's declining health, Borges found employment in 1937 as an assistant librarian at the Miguel Cané Municipal Library where he remained until 1946. In February of 1938, the senior Borges died. During Christmas of that same year, Borges became gravely ill from septicemia, resulting from an accident provoked by his poor vision. During his convalescence in 1939, Borges wrote the beguiling story of "Pierre Menard, autor del *Quijote*" ("Pierre Menard, Author of *Don Quixote*") to prove to himself that he was still sane. His literary production continued in earnest, and in 1940, in collaboration with Silvina Ocampo and Adolfo Bioy Casares, Borges edited his *Antología de la literatura fantástica (Anthology of Fantastic Literature)*. In 1941, the *Sur* publishing house released his second book of stories *El jardín de los senderos que se bifurcan (The Garden of Forking Paths)*. That same year, Borges used one of his several pseudonyms—Bustos Domecq—when he collaborated with Bioy Casares on a series of detective stories entitled *Seis problemas para don Isidro Parodi (Six Problems for Don Isidro Parodi)*. Then in 1944 *Sur* published Borges's most famous collection of stories, *Ficciones*, composed of stories from *El jardín de los senderos que se bifurcan (The Garden of Forking Paths)* and *Artificios (Artifices)*. In recognition of Borges achievement, the Argentine Society of Writers created and awarded the Grand Honorary Prize for this collection.

Politics played a role in the literary and family life of Borges when, in 1946, Borges's position at the library was changed to "Inspector of Poultry" by the Perón Government—an action taken to reprimand Borges for having signed declarations against the Fascist regime. Borges then resigned his political appointment to begin a career as a public speaker, after which the Perón government sent a policeman to takes notes at Borges's lectures. At this time, Borges became editor of a new magazine, *Los anales de Buenos Aires* (*The Annals of Buenos Aires*). While in this position, Borges introduced many new writers to the public, among them Julio Cortázar and Felisberto Hernández. In 1948, Borges's mother and sister were imprisoned for demonstrating against Perón. While his mother was allowed to remain under house arrest, his sister Norah completed her sentence in a local prison.

During the 1950s, Borges further solidified his scholarly and literary career when in 1950 he was appointed president of the Argentine Society of Writers. The next year, he collaborated with Bioy Casares on a second anthology, *Los mejores cuentos policiales* (*The Best Detective Stories*). His most popular book of essays, *Otras inquisiciones* (*Other Inquisitions*), was published in 1952. When the Córdoba revolution ousted the Peron regeim in 1955, Borges was appointed Director of the National Library. In 1956 Borges received the first of many honorary doctorates from the University of Cuyo in Argentina, and became Professor of English and American Literature at the University of Buenos Aries. That same year he won the National Prize for Literature.

The 1960s marked Borges's arrival on the international scene. Borges published *El Hacedor* in 1960, later entitled *Dreamtigers* in its English translation, and in 1961, he received the Formentor International Publishers Prize. In 1962 Borges's works appeared in English for the first time in book form as *Labyrinths: Selected Stories and Other Writings*. France awarded Borges the Order of Arts and Letters and Argentina appointed him to the Academy of Letters. In 1965, Ana María Barrenchea published the first critical study in English of Borges's work. In the same year, Borges received the Order of the British Empire. In 1967, Borges married Elsa Astete Millán, a recently widowed childhood friend. The couple divorced three years later. In 1969, Holt Rinehart published Richard Burgin's

Conversations with Jorge Luis Borges, a book-length series of interviews in English, while at the same time, E. P. Dutton began work on the publication of Borges's complete works in English.

Borges was received and honored by many countries and distinguished academic institutions during the 1970s and the early 1980s. He received honorary doctorates from Columbia University in 1971 and one from Harvard University 10 years later. With the return of Juan Peron as Argentina's recently elected president in 1973, Borges resigned from his directorship of the National Library. In 1975 Borges published his final collection of stories, *El libro de arena* (*The Book of Sand*), but also suffered the loss of his mother who had lived to the age of 99. From 1975 on, María Kodama, his secretary and friend, regularly accompanied Borges on his travels, and in 1977, again with Bioy Casares, Borges published *Nuevos cuentos de Bustos Domecq* (*New Bustos Domecq Stories*). In 1980, the King and Queen of Spain received Borges at court and awarded him the Cervantes Prize, and in 1983, François Mitterand, president of France, awarded Jorge Luis Borges the Legion d'Honneurr. On April 26, 1986, Borges married María Kodama. On June 14 of that same year Jorge Luis Borges died from liver cancer in Geneva. Borges was laid to rest, as he wished, in the Pleinpalais cemetery.

PLOT SUMMARY OF
"Death and the Compass"

Appearing in 1942 as "La muerte y la brújula," Borges dedicated this story to Mandie Molina Vedia.

Quotations from "Death and the Compass" in Borges, Jorge Luis. *The Aleph and Other Stories: 1933-1969.* ed. and trans. Norman Thomas di Giovanni. (New York: E. P. Dutton & Co., Inc., 1970): pp. 65-78.

This detective story replete with clues involving numbers, colors, and compass points centers on a detective tracking a crime spree as if he were an adventurer caught in a jungle of textual signs and metaphors. Three murders take place.

   The first occurs in the strange and disconcerting Hotel du Nord on the third of December. Rabbi Marcel Yarmolinsky occupies a room on floor R opposite the room of the Tetrarch of Galilee. He is staying at the hotel while attending the Third Talmudic Congress as a delegate from Podolsk. Little is known about the rabbi other than that he is traveling with his complete works; many scholarly tomes covering subjects such as the Kabbalah, the Hasidic sect, and the names of God in the Pentateuch are found in his room when, on December fourth, he is discovered murdered. Inspector Treviranus decides almost immediately that the rabbi died in a failed effort to steal the sapphires owned by the Tetrarch. In sharp contrast, Detective Lönnrot, intrigued by the collection of books in the rabbi's room, suggests a rabbinical explanation to the murder after discovering a dead rabbit in the room. In the meantime, an editor from the *Judische Zeitung*, on the scene to cover the murder, interrupts their discussion on the possible Jewish superstitions at play. Another policeman discovers that Yarmolinsky's typewriter holds a paper with a cryptic message: "The first letter of the Name has been uttered." (67) This finding convinces Lönnrot that his theory is correct and he carries off the rabbi's books for further study. During his examination of the scholarly works, Lönnrot comes to focus his attention on the Tetragrammaton, the 100th and unspeakable name for God. The editor from the *Judische Zeitung* interviews Lönnrot during his investigation and later reports that the detective "had taken up the study of the names of God in order to find out the name of the murderer." (68)

The second murder happens a month later on the third of January in a very seedy part on the western side of town. Again the victim is found with a deep knife wound but this time on the floor of a dilapidated hardware store. The policemen on duty note that some letters are scrawled on the wall in chalk where red and yellow diamond shapes were once painted. By the time Treviranus and Lönnrot arrive on the scene, the dead man has been identified as Daniel Simon Azevedo, known to be a thief and an informer. The words on the wall are: "The second letter of the Name has been uttered." (69) Lönnrot apparently dismisses the fact that Azevedo is connected with a known and dangerous criminal, Red Scharlach, nicknamed Scharlach the Dandy.

On the night of the third of February, the third crime takes place. That evening Inspector Treviranus receives a call, abruptly cut off, by a man called Ginzberg or Ginsberg saying that he has facts related to the "double sacrifice of Azevedo and Yarmolinsky." (69) Treviranus determines that the call came from a waterfront tavern. The owner, Black Finnegan, tells the inspector about a boarder named Gryphius who had used the phone in his office. Finnegan recounts that soon after the call, a coach arrived at the tavern with two men dressed as harlequins—in costumes of red, green, and yellow—who greeted Gryphius and spoke to him in Yiddish before going up to his room. Apparently drunk, all three left the tavern shortly thereafter. As they left, one of the harlequins wrote some words on a sign nearby. When Treviranus looked, he read: "The last letter of the Name has been uttered." (71) In Gryphius's tiny room, Treviranus found blood on the floor and a book in Latin in the closet. He called in Lönnrot who paid no attention to the witnesses that Treviranus had gathered but spent his time reading the book, a 1739 edition of Leusden's *Philologus Hebraeo-Graecus*. Treviranus in his usual grounded fashion posed the theory that the events of the evening were a "put-up job." (71) But Lönnrot kept to his academic hypothesis and read to the inspector an underlined passage from the book: "the Jewish day begins at sundown and ends the following sundown" (71) and suggested to Treviranus that this passage and the

17

word "sacrifice" in the interrupted phone message were the most important clues regarding this and the two previous crimes.

On March 1st, Inspector Treviranus opened a large sealed envelope in which he found a letter from a "Baruch Spinoza" pointing out that the crime spree would be limited to three because the location of each murder formed a perfect triangle on the city map included in the envelope. Lönnrot later studied the materials—measuring the triangle with a compass—and concluded that the crimes shared a symmetry in time—occurring on the third of the months of December, January, and February—as well as in space—in the north, west, and east of the town. From this conclusion, Lönnrot announced to Treviranus with complete certainty that by the following day the criminals would be in custody because he was sure they planned a fourth crime. Shortly after speaking with Treviranus, Lönnrot boarded a train for a deserted villa to the south called Triste-le-Roy. Here suddenly the narrator's voice is present again, silent since the opening of the story, as it describes the landscape "to the south of the city of my story" (73) as having a dark polluted river and a factory suburb where thugs thrive. This is just the place for criminals such as Azevedo or Scharlach. As Lönnrot traveled, he wondered if Scharlach was the intended fourth victim. He reflected on the three months of work it had cost him to reach his conclusions based on the clues from the triangle and the recently acquired word 'Tetragrammaton'. Now the mystery surrounding the crimes seemed all too clear to Lönnrot

On March 1st, Inspector Treviranus opened a large sealed envelope in which he found a letter from a "Baruch Spinoza" pointing out that the crime spree would be limited to three because the location of each murder formed a perfect triangle on the city map included in the envelope. Lönnrot later studied the materials—measuring the triangle with a compass—and concluded that the crimes shared a symmetry in time—occurring on the third of the months of December, January, and February—as well as in space—in the north, west, and east of the town. From this conclusion, Lönnrot announced to Treviranus with complete certainty that by the following day the criminals would be in custody because he was sure they planned a fourth crime. Shortly after speaking with Treviranus, Lönnrot boarded a train for a deserted villa to the south called

Triste-le-Roy. Here suddenly the narrator's voice is present again, silent since the opening of the story, as it describes the landscape "to the south of the city of my story" (73) as having a dark polluted river and a factory suburb where thugs thrive. This is just the place for criminals such as Azevedo or Scharlach. As Lönnrot traveled, he wondered if Scharlach was the intended fourth victim. He reflected on the three months of work it had cost him to reach his conclusions based on the clues from the triangle and the recently acquired word 'Tetragrammaton'. Now the mystery surrounding the crimes seemed all too clear to Lönnrot as he got off at the deserted platform.

While walking, Lönnrot noticed the "rectangular mirador of villa Triste-le-Roy" (74), the irregular perimeter, the eucalyptus trees, and the symmetries in the architecture of the building. Receptive statues of the Greek gods Diana and Hermes in the grounds bothered Lönnrot as he entered the villa. Inside, though not large, the house too held repeating structures of angles, staircases, and mirrors. Climbing to the third and last floor, he reached the mirador where Lönnrot noticed the moonlight penetrating diamond-shaped windows of red, green, and yellow. Suddenly two men grabbed and disarmed him. A third said: "You are very kind. You've saved us a night and a day." It was Scharlach. Almost dumbfounded, Lönnrot asked him if he too was after the 'Secret Name.' To which Red Scharlach replied simply: "No… I'm after something more ephemeral, more frail. I'm after Erik Lönnrot." (75)

In a numerically charged explanation of his motive, Scharlach recounts to Lönnrot that three years earlier Lönnrot arrested Scharlach's brother in a skirmish in which Scharlach was seriously injured. His men helped him escape to Triste-le-Roy where he spent nine days and nine nights recovering from his wounds. In his feverish state, he obsessed on the statue of Janus in the villa's grounds: "I came to loathe my body, I came to feel that two eyes, two hands, two lungs, are as monstrous as two faces. . . . During those nights, I swore by the god who looks with two faces and by all the gods of fever and of mirrors that I would weave a maze around the man who sent my brother to prison. Well, I have woven it. . . . Its materials are a dead rabbit, a compass, an eighteenth-century sect, a Greek word, a dagger, and the diamond-shaped patterns on a paint-store wall." (76)

Scharlach then recounted how chance helped him construct his maze. By design, he had sent Azevedo to steal the Tetrarch's sapphires but Azevedo betrayed him and spoiled the plan by murdering the rabbi. Scharlach read Lönnrot's theories in the *Judische Zeitung*. The suggestion that the Hasidim had sacrificed the rabbi for his books about the Secret Name gave Scharlach the idea to continue the "sacrifices" by planning his revenge and murder of Azevedo a month later. The third crime in the following month was a ruse since Gryphius-Ginzberg-Ginsberg was Scharlach aided by his men to create the impression that another murder had been committed. He then told Lönnrot that he counted on the detective's logicial prowess to deduce that the three crimes would really foretell a fourth because the Tetragammaton, that is the Name of God, has four letters. For this reason, Scharlach had underlined the passage in the Leusden edition to lure Lönnrot to the isolated villa.

While Lönnrot listened, he stared at the red, green, and, yellow windows. Ever the logician, Lönnrot then pointed out to Scharlach the flaw in the construction of his murderous maze. "*The next time I kill you*, said Scharlach, *I promise you such a maze, which is made up of a single straight line and which is invisible and unending*. He moved back a few steps. Then, taking careful aim, he fired." (78)

LIST OF CHARACTERS IN
"Death and the Compass"

Erik Lönnrot: A would-be logician, Detective Lönnrot insists from the beginning that the first murder is more than mere mishap. Lönnrot uses the murdered Rabbi's collection of books to construct a scholarly theory to explain the series of murders that follow. This theory eventually proves to be disastrously mistaken.

Rabbi Marcel Yarmolinsky: The first murder victim is killed in his room at the Hotel du Nord. He is a delegate to the Third Talmudic Congress who travels with many heavy religious and philosophical tomes.

Red Scharlach, nicknamed Scharlach the Dandy: Scharlach is a gangster who has sworn to "get" Lönnrot. As it turns out, his intricate plan to do so involves another thug who turns traitor, a pair of accomplices, three murders, and a cunning plan that fools his intended victim.

Inspector Treviranus: A cigar-smoking policeman who prefers the harsh reality of clues to Lönnrot's complicated academic theories, Treviranus is convinced that the murder of the Rabbi was a bungled attempt to steal the sapphires of a rich man in the next hotel room. A Christian, Treviranus reminds Lönnrot none of his theories based on Talmudic texts makes any sense to him.

An editor from the *Judische Zeitung*: Though never named, the editor appears at every crime scene and is responsible for a thorough coverage of the series of murders including mentioning Lönnrot's study of the names of God to solve the crimes.

Daniel Simon Azevedo: A man with a reputation as a thug, Azevedo is meant to steal sapphires from the Tetrarch of Galilee, staying in the room next to Rabbi Yarmolinsky. Instead, he kills the Rabbi and later is found murdered on a seedy side of town.

Ginzberg-Ginsburg-Gryphius: Staying in a room above a bar owned by Black Finnegan, this man has little contact with anyone but does make a call to the police foretelling the next crime. In what turns out to be a charade, he is allegedly kidnapped and murdered by two men dressed as harlequins.

Black Finnegan: Owner of a tavern called the Liverpool House, catering to sailors. Finnegan recounts to Treviranus the events surrounding the disappearance of a boarder named Gryphius.

CRITICAL VIEWS ON
"Death and the Compass"

JORGE LUIS BORGES ON THE STORY

[In this fragment, Borges identifies places in Buenos Aires corresponding to place names in "La muerte y la brújula" ("Death and the Compass"). His naming of the story's characters and his use of shapes and colors also figure here. Borges recognizes the Jewish elements in the story and explains his repetition of the Kabbalah as his way of intensifying the sense of mystery.]

Since 1923, I had been doing my best to be the poet of Buenos Aires and never quite succeeding. When, in 1942, I undertook a nightmare version of the city in "Death and the Compass," my friends told me that at long last I had managed to evoke a sufficiently recognizable image of my home town. A few topographical elucidations may perhaps be in order. The Hôtel du Nord stands for the Plaza Hotel. The estuary is the Río de la Plata, called "the great lion-colored river" by Lugones, and, far more effectively, "the unmoving river" by Eduardo Mallea. The Rue de Toulon is the Paseo Colón, or rather, in terms of rowdiness, the old Paseo de Julio, today called Leandro Alem. Triste-le-Roy, a beautiful name invented by Amanda Molina Vedia, stands for the now demolished Hotel Las Delicias in Adrogué. (Amanda had painted a map of an imaginary island on the wall of her bedroom; on her map I discovered the name Triste-le-Roy.) In order to avoid any suspicion of realism, I used distorted names and placed the story in some cosmopolitan setting beyond any specific geography. The characters' names further bear this out: Treviranus is German, Azevedo is Portuguese and Jewish, Yarmolinsky is a Polish Jew, Finnegan is Irish, Lönnrot is Swedish.

Patterns in time and space are to be found throughout the story. A triangle is suggested but the solution is really based on a rhombus. This rhombus is picked up in the Carnival costumes of the seeming kidnappers and in the windows of Triste-le-Roy, as well as in the Fourfold Name of God, the Tetragrammaton. A thread of red also runs through the story's pages. There is the sunset on the rose-colored wall and, in the same scene, the blood splashed on the dead man's face. Red is found in the detective's and in the gunman's names.

The killer and the slain, whose minds work in the same way, may be the same man. Lönnrot is not an unbelievable fool walking into his own death trap but, in a symbolic way, a man committing suicide. This is hinted at by the similarity of their names. The end syllable of Lönnrot means red in German, and Red Scharlach is also translatable, in German, as Red Scarlet.

No apology is needed for repeated mention of the Kabbalah, for it provides the reader and the all-too-subtle detective with a false track, and the story is, as most of the names imply, a Jewish one. The Kabbalah also provides an additional sense of mystery.

> —Jorge Luis Borges, *The Aleph and Other Stories: 1933-1969.* ed. and trans. Norman Thomas di Giovanni. (New York: E. P. Dutton Co., Inc., 1970): pp. 268-9.

EDNA AIZENBERG ON JEWISH ELEMENTS AND SPINOZA

> [Editor of *Borges and His Successors: The Borgesian Impact on Literature and the Arts* (1990) and the author of extensive essays on Borges, the Kabbalah, and postcolonial literature, Professor Aizenberg examines several of the Jewish elements she finds present in the texts of Borges. In particular, Aizenberg finds most important the "Jew-as-Intellect" because she believes Borges privileges "mental virtues and spiritual labyrinths." In this excerpt, Professor Aizenberg examines Lönnrot as the Spinoza figure in "La muerte y la brújula" ("Death and the Compass").]

One of the essential ways in which "La muerte y la brújula" must be read, then, is as an opening up by Borges of a consecrated literary mode. But such a reading does not exhaust the fiction's possibilities. Because the tale is—in Borges's own description—"a Jewish one," with a plot constructed out of the stuff of Jewish mysticism and philosophy, with comments deriding the kind of anti-Semitism rampant at the time, and with Jews and Hebraists exercising their intelligence, it can likewise be read as yet another salute by the author to Hitler's hated Jew-as-Mind. "La muerte y la brújula" is, in fact, a version and perversion of certain schemes produced by that mind as part of the impossible, but inevitable human struggle to comprehend the universe. In the fiction, Borges pays tribute to—even as he exposes the limitations of—Baruch Spinoza's rational-geometric elucidation of God, humanity and cosmos. Through an homage which is at the same time a challenge, he shows his debt to this incarnation of the intellectual Jew archetype, a thinker who, he says, has greatly influenced his work.

The Spinoza (or Spinozist) in "La muerte y la brújula" is Erik Lönnrot. He is the detective attempting to solve the series of three murders occurring in a nightmare version of Buenos Aires which forms the core of the story's plot. Lönnrot is what the Nazis would have called a *weisser Jude*: an intellectual; a man unafraid [to] become a Hebraist in order to carry out his investigation (*OC*, 500); someone who shows respect for Jewish belief and appreciation for rabbinic and kabbalistic writings. (This, in contrast to his colleague, the probably not-insignificantly Germanic Inspector Franz Treviranus, who is repulsed by intellectualism and Judaic literature.) Lönnrot's connection to the philosopher for whom, as Borges notes, the universe was logical and hence capable of rational explanation is insinuated in "La muerte y la brújula" through a number of hints ("Baruch Spinoza," *Conferencia*s, p. 107). The most obvious of these, appearing towards the middle of the story, is a letter signed "Baruj Spinoza" [sic] which is received by Treviranus, but is clearly intended for Lönnrot, who alone seems to understand it. This obvious clue serves to supplement and confirm others, which begin to appear in the narration right from the outset.

In the first paragraph the reader is told that Lönnrot prides himself on being a "pure reasoner" (*OC*, 499). This means that he tries to puzzle out the solutions to mysteries such as the one before him through abstract reasoning, ignoring "mere circumstances"—empirical evidence which is not logically deduced—and instead seeking a rational explanation for, or an organized pattern in the events (*OC*, 504). Lönnrot makes this approach of a pure logician—Spinoza's approach—clear in an exchange with Treviranus after the first killing in the series, that of the rabbi and Talmudist, Marcelo Yarmolinsky. When the inspector, the antagonist of Judaic mental constructs, suggests that the homicide may have been quite simply an error, with Yarmolinsky the unwitting victim of a jewel thief who entered his hotel suite by mistake, Lönnrot retorts that his hypothesis is too fraught with chance. The death of a rabbi requires a purely rabbinic—logical, Talmudic—explanation, not the imaginary misadventures of some imaginary robber (*OC*, 500).

Lönnrot's argument is Spinozist in its insistence that knowledge—finding out who the murderer is—can be derived from a coherent structure of premises and conclusions based on reason, and not on un-reason: improvisation, chance, circumstancial evidence and, above all, the imagination. As G. H. R. Parkinson writes in his *Spinoza's Theory of Knowledge*:

> [The philosopher believed that the] ... search for truth was to be put upon a new and sound basis; men were no longer to go about their researches in a more or less haphazard manner, but were to do so methodically, in accordance with some plan.

This plan or method, Parkinson goes on, was rooted in "the assumption that knowledge constitutes a deductive system" (p.13). The information and ideas on which such a system was to be built could be provided only by "pure reason" (p. 15), since Spinoza considered "the imagination [the name he gave to cognition not rationally deduced] to be defective as a means of knowledge" (p. 156).

The Spinozism of Lönnrot's search for truth becomes even clearer when Borges intimates that not only its method (reason), but also its goal corresponds to the philosopher's: to reach God, who in the story as in Spinoza's system represents complete understanding of the universe under the aspect of eternity. Borges suggests this correspondence by establishing a link between the name of the assassin Lönnrot is pursuing and the ineffable Name of God (*OC*, 501; 504). At the site of each of the three homicides the pure logician is investigating, a clue is left which seems to relate the killing to a search by a Jewish sect for God's secret Name. Lönnrot, convinced that by following this lead he would discover the identity (name) of the criminal, himself becomes one of the "seekers of the Name," in effect, a seeker of God (*OC*, 501). That his pursuit is synonymous with a pursuit of complete understanding of the universe under the aspect of eternity is made evident when Borges explains that the hidden Name Lönnrot is after contains God's ninth attribute, eternity, that is, immediate knowledge of all past, present and future things (*OC*, 501). It is also made evident by the fact that when Lönnrot finally finds his "God," under the guise of the gangster Red Scharlach (who is of Jewish background, like the Judeo-Christian Lord, and inhabits the Southside, the blurry frontier of the city which in Borges's works connotes the frontier of the soul), he learns that this deity is in fact characterized by eternity and omniscience: he has emotions as wide as the endless, eternal cosmos, and knows unpublicized, hidden details about the murders and the investigation that only an all-seeing being could know (Gallagher, p. 102). (…)

Borges's Spinoza, Erik Lönnrot, does not find Meaning; neither does he achieve blessedness, the contented life the philosopher believed would flow from a rational understanding of Nature. Instead of guiding him to knowledge and happiness, pure logic confronts him with error and death: his reasoned deductions do not provide the solution to the mystery since they are to a large extent wrong; and the geometry of the divine he has followed does not map out a path to a rational god who endows man with infinite wisdom, but rather to an irrational deity who weaves a labyrinth, a death trap, for those mortals presumptuous enough to believe that their intellect can pierce the great *ignoramus*.

But even if Spinoza's scheme, Lönnrot's scheme, fails as an absolute explanation of the Absolute, it succeeds as a provisional explanation, the only type available to humankind. That is why in "La muerte y la brújula" Borges *does* give his Spinozist detective credit for his keenness of mind and for his partial, approximate penetration of the enigma (*OC*, 499). That is why, too, he repeatedly invokes Spinoza's masterful name, lauding this incarnation of the Jew-as-Intellect, who despite his very human nothingness took on the Infinite, producing a brilliant geometry which may not explain God or Nature, but which may help people bear its impenetrability (*OC*, 200). That is why, in the final analysis, he admires all the personifications of the Jew-as-Mind mentioned here. For each, descended from those who created one of the essential human schemes sustaining Western woman in her confrontation with God's secret dictionary (*OC*, 708), himself created some admirable scheme—a literature crafted out of dreams, a poetry of images and melodies—which imposes temporary order and gives comfort in the face of the chaotic and the unintelligible.

> —Edna Aizenberg, "The Diverse Intonation of Some Jewish Metaphors," *The Aleph Weaver: Biblical, Kabbalistic and Judaic Elements in Borges*. (Potomac, Maryland: Scripta Humanistica, 1984): pp. 131-5, 137-8.

HAROLD BLOOM ON AESTHETIC MOTIVATIONS

[Sterling Professor of Humanities at Yale University and Berg Professor of English at New York University, Harold Bloom is the author of 20 books and the editor of many more. Commenting on his favorite Borges stories, Professor Bloom acknowledges, like many others, the palpable presence of literary influences in the tale. Bloom believes, as he mentions in this excerpt, that Borges's motivations are neither religious nor philosophical but rather aesthetic.]

Of all Borges' stories, the one I loved best thirty years ago is still my favorite: "Death and the Compass." Like almost all of his work, it is intensely literary: it knows and declares its belatedness, the contingency that governs its relationship with previous literature. Borges' paternal grandmother was English; his father's library was large and centered on English literature. In Borges we have the anomaly of a Hispanic writer who first read *Don Quixote* in English translation, and whose literary culture, though universal, remained English and North American in its deeper sensibility. Still Borges, oriented toward a literary career, was haunted by the military glory that had dominated both his father's and his mother's families. Inheriting the poor eyesight that had kept his father from becoming an officer, Borges seems to have inherited also his father's flight into the library as a refuge in which dreaming could atone for an impossible life of action. What Ellmann said of the Shakespeare-obsessed Joyce, that he was anxious only to incorporate as many influences as possible, seems much truer of Borges, who overtly absorbs and then deliberately reflects the entire canonical tradition. Whether this open embrace of his precursors finally curtailed Borges' achievement is a difficult question, which I hope to begin to answer later in this chapter.

Master of labyrinths and of mirrors, Borges was a profound student of literary influence, and as a skeptic who cared more for imaginative literature than for religion or philosophy, he taught us how to read such speculations primarily for their aesthetic value. His curious fate as a writer, and as the foremost inaugurator of modern Latin American literature, cannot be separated from either his aesthetic universalism or what I suppose must be called his aesthetic aggressiveness. Rereading him now, I am both charmed and cheered, more even than I was thirty years ago, because his political anarchism (of his father's rather mild variety) is so refreshing at a time when the study of literature has become wholly politicized, and one fears the increasing politicization of literature itself.

>—Harold Bloom, "Borges, Neruda, and Pessoa: Hispanic-Portugues Whitman," *The Western Canon: The Books and School of the Ages.* (New York: Harcourt Brace & Company, 1994): pp: 464-5.

CARLOS FUENTES ON CITY AND FICTION

> [Carlos Fuentes is one of the most widely published Latin American writers in English. His work has been translated into 23 other languages. English translations of his novels include *Where the Air Is Clear* (1960), *The Death of Artemio Cruz* (1964), *Terra Nostra* (1972), and *The Old Gringo* (1986). His long story *Aura* was translated into English in 1966. The recipient of the Cervantes Prize, Carlos Fuentes currently has homes in Mexico City and London. The present lecture was delivered to the Royal Society of Arts in London in November 1990. In this excerpt, Fuentes attributes the widely used relationship of city and its fiction in Latin American literature to Borges and in particular to the story "Death and the Compass."]

The relationship between a city and its fiction, then, can come from a presence as material and direct as those of Pablo Neruda and Luis Rafael Sánchez, or from an absence as physical as those of César Aira and Héctor Libertella or as metaphysical as that of Adolfo Bioy-Casares or as ghostly as that of José Bianco or as deadly as that of Osvaldo Soriano and Luisa Valenzuela or as hopefully critical and creative as that of Julio Cortázar. But all of these strains really originate (in their modern mode) in Borges himself and, I dare say, in a single brief story, 'Death and the Compass', where in a few pages the author gives us a city of dream and death, absence and violence, murder and disappearance, language and silence. How does he do this?

Borges describes death as the opportunity to rediscover all the instants of our life and combine them freely as dreams. We can do this, he adds, with the co-operation of God, our friends, and William Shakespeare. If it is dream that finally defeats death by giving form to all these instants liberated by death itself, Borges naturally uses the oneiric to render his deepest vision of the city of Buenos Aires. In 'Death and the Compass', Buenos Aires is never mentioned, but the story is Borges's most poetic vision of his native city, far more so than the more naturalistic approach of a tale like 'Street-corner Man'. The author himself explains that

> 'Death and the Compass' is a kind of nightmare, a nightmare in which there are elements of Buenos Aires, deformed by the horror of the nightmare. There I think of the Paseo Colón and call it Rue de Toulon; I think of the country houses of Adrogué and call them Triste-le-Roy. When this story was published, my friends told me that at last they had found in what I wrote the flavour of the outskirts of Buenos Aires. Precisely because I had not set out to find that flavour, because I had abandoned myself to a dream, I was able to accomplish, after so many years, what I had previously sought in vain …

Buenos Aires is what he had sought, and his first book of poems tells us how he had sought it, fervently—*Fervor de Buenos Aires*. But the reality of Buenos Aires had only come, in the end, through a dream—that is, through the imagination. I, too, had searched for that city while reading Borges as a very young man and found it only, like Borges himself, in these words from 'Death and the Compass': 'The train came to a stop at a deserted loading platform. Lönnrot got off. It was one of those forlorn evenings that seem as empty as dawn.' The metaphor, when I read it, became the epitaph of my own relationship with Buenos Aires. It was a delicate, fugitive moment, as James Joyce would say, a sudden spiritual reality that appears in the midst of the most memorable or the most commonplace of our days but that is always fragile and passing. I cling to this epiphany, even while saying that through these Argentine authors, Aira, Bianco, Borges, Bioy, and Cortázar, I understand that presence may well be a dream, that dream is a fiction, and that history can begin anew from an absence.

Argentine fiction is, on the whole, the richest in Spanish America. Perhaps this is due to the clamour for putting things into words that I mentioned earlier. But by demanding words, the writers of the River Plate create a second history, as valid as—perhaps even more valid than—the real one. This is what Borges accomplishes in 'Death and the Compass', and it makes us wonder and wander further into his work.

> —Carlos Fuentes, "The Accidents of Time," *The Borges Tradition.* ed. Norman Thomas di Giovanni, (London: Constable, 1995): pp. 60-62.

JORGE HERNÁNDEZ MARTÍN ON DETECTIVE FICTION

> [Professor Hernández Martín has published several critical essays on the detective genre as well as the works of Miguel González Prando and Rafael V. Blanco. In the present work, Hernández Martín analyzes the detective stories of Borges and his alter-ego Bustos Domecq along with *The Name of the Rose* by Umberto Eco. In this excerpt, Professor Hernández Martín considers the interchanges at play between investigator/criminal and reader/author.]

In "Death and the Compass," the investigator and the criminal play out the game of difference between the reader and the author over the text of the crime. In order to snare the detective, the criminal, aware of the line of inquiry taken by the investigator, will lay out clues from which the detective will develop the detectory schema. The criminal's motivation in this case is revenge. It is not unusual to find this kind of battle of wits in a detective story. Ever since Dupin's confrontation with Minister D—in "The Purloined Letter," criminals and detectives have shared an uneasy distinction within the genre. For example, both have inordinate pride—criminals' pride in their ability leads them to commit a crime deviously plotted and enacted, while detectives are proud of their power to conceive of the way the fiendish plot was conocted and carried out by conjectural means. Both detectives and criminals are not beyond breaking the law, which is understandable enough in the case of the criminal, but which seems peculiar in the case of the detective, who is the agent of order in the text. The detective and the criminal seem mysterious and cryptic in their deeds and pronouncements, especially to the reader, who is kept at a distance for the purposes of delay and misdirection in both the criminal's and the detective's case. Detectives, finally, have the godlike power to judge and punish, which they wield over the other characters in the fiction; criminals are similarly godlike (one might say demonic) in the way they dispose of human life and property with motives that are apparently beyond understanding.

The detective and the criminal, conjointly, are a source of wonder for the reader. Borges's story problematizes the pragmatic strategy demanded of the reader by detective narratives: A rabbi lies murdered in his room at the Hôtel du Nord where he was lodged as delegate to a Talmudic conference taking place in the (unnamed) city. Borges has acknowledged that the fictional city that appears in "Death and the Compass" follows the spatial disposition of Buenos Aires. The abandoned villa of Triste-le-Roy, for example, where the denouement takes place "stands for the now demolished Hotel Las Delicias in Adrogué...ten or fifteen minutes south of Buenos Aires" (*The Aleph* 263). More important than the fictional reflection of the author's private maze is the fact that Borges uses the procedure employed by Poe to mask the site of an actual crime in "The Mystery of Marie Rogêt." In Borges's hands the technique yields startling results. Poe places a crime occurring in New York, and reported by local newspapers, in Paris. Borges places a crime that has not happened (a fictional crime) in a city disguised as somewhere else. Regardless of the name the reader might choose for the fictional city—Buenos Aires, London, Montevideo, Paris, Prague—Borges's fictional city suggests another place by the shortcomings of the reader's association.

> —Jorge Hernández Martín, "'Death and the Compass': Lönnrot's Last Case?" *Readers and Labyrinths,* (New York: Garland, 1995): pp. 79-81.

SVEND ØSTERGÅRD ON REPRESENTATION

[Professor Østergård is the author of several critical studies on semiotics, as well as on the role of narrator and authorship in narrative structures. In this article, Professor Østergård posits that reality is based on situations stabilized between objects and events. In Borges's texts, however, Østergård believes that no such stability is present. Rather, circumstances arising between representation and the represented dissolves into destabilization. This excerpt offers two perspectives of the accidental killing of the rabbi in "La muerte y la brújula" ("Death and the Compass").]

a) The first killing was accidental. A burglar got lost in the hotel and stumbled into the room of the rabbi. At this pure descriptive level the event turns out to be fatal, it just happens, only subjected to the logic of action (it is stressed that the burglar acted instinctively and that in this instinct half a century of violence was hidden). To this level of fatality the fiction contrasts the discourse of Lönnrot. He seeks an argumentative and logical coherence in the circumstances of the event. He seeks a discursive explanation in the sense that he looks for an answer in the discourse of the cabbalism (*"Suddenly (he) become a bibliophile or Hebraist . . ."*). We can say that we here have two different temporal chains of events converging and bifurcating around the same event. On the one hand, the cause of the killing is submerged into an infinite web of infinitesimal causes. Some of these can not be reconstructed at all, they are immersed into *"half a century of violence,"* some can afterwards be reconstructed but appear totally fatal, as for example placing the room of the rabbi on the same floor as the owner of the finest sapphires in the world. These untraceable series of events have a form which we can qualify as the *temporal form of reality*. On the other hand, according to Lönnrot's conjecture, the killing is one definite term in a precisely defined series of events. Moreover, this series is not determined through the immanent logic of the act but through a transcendental logic, which is located in a text. The acts *represent* the logic of the text. The fiction deals with representation, but representation works in a twofold way: The series of killings which Lönnrot predicted were supposed to represent the secrete name of God, moreover, the construction he made is a formal representation of an internal coherence in the circumstances of the events. In this perspective we can say that the series of events have a form which we can qualify as the *temporal form of representation*.

b) Lönnrot's reconstruction did not change the circumstances of the event itself, but it *did* change the effects of the event. That is, the mere fact that he made a formal representation of the real-time causal chain of events emanating from the killing of the rabbi changed this chain. This we could call a *principle of complementarity* between the real-time causal chain and the representation of it.

The murder of the rabbi was something which just happened in the world and thereby caused the conjecture of Lönnrot. Similarly, on a superior level we can say that also Lönnrot's intervention just happened, because on the discursive level it appears as that *chance* which Scharlach had waited for and which caused him to arrange the subsequent series of events. The murderer acted according to an instinct which was immersed into centuries of violence, but in the same manner Lönnrot reasoned according to an instinct which was immersed into a (unconscious) disposition for symmetries and order (*"A set of callipers and a compass completed his quick intuition"*). In the same way as the murder is the object of Lönnrot's investigation, Lönnrot's own style of interpretation is the object of Red Scharlachs intervention. Lönnrot wants to expel the element of chance from the level of the act (*"In the hypothesis that you propose chance intervenes copiously,"* he says to Treviranus), but he does not see that his own intervention is an element of chance.

The object of the investigation and the investigation itself are connected in a möbius-like manner. Scharlach predicted Lönnrot's conjecture and he arranged events in the world that confirmed this conjecture. But this means that the conjecture of Lönnrot was already a part of the universe towards which the conjecture was directed. He was not just investigating the world but also his own (unconscious) style of investigating. Lönnrot forgot that his own style of reasoning was a part of the real-time series of events, and therefore his style of reasoning was a subset of the sequence of events which he reconstructed through a logical interpretation. This of course leads to an infinite regress: *his style of reasoning leads to his interpretation of the events which as a subset contains his style of reasoning which leads to his interpretation which...etc.* It is this fact which appears in the descriptive parts of the fiction, which abound in symmetries, mirrors, reflections, duplications, infinities (*"he was multiplied infinitely in opposing mirrors"*).

—Svend Østergård, "The Unconscious of Representation," *Variaciones Borges* 1 (1996): pp. 107-8.

FLOYD MERRELL ON LABYRINTHS AND THE STORY

[Professor in the Department of Languages and Literature at Purdue University, Merrell's most recent books include *Unthinking Thinking: Jorge Luis Borges, Mathematics, and the "New Physics"* (1991) and *Sensing Semiosis: Toward the Possibility of Complementary Cultural "Logics"* (1998). In the present essay, Professor Merrell reflects on concepts such as Newtonian mechanics and asymmetrical confusions in texts by Calvino and Borges as he constructs arguments using mathematics and physics. This excerpt concentrates on the labyrinths of logic created by Lönnrot in "Death and the Compass."]

Speaking of labyrinths, consider Borges' Lönnrot, of "Death and the Compass" (1962: 76-87). Lönnrot the supercogitating detective, thought he had things all wrapped up in a tidy package. By way of an intricately complex interplay of *simples*—a well-reasoned combination of threes and fours, a harmony of time and space symmetries, logical inferences derived from the Judaeo-Christian tradition, and the regularities of human behavior reduced to a minimum— Lönnrot had determined precisely when and where a fourth murder was to occur, even though the assassin himself had predicated its non-occurrence. There, according to Lönnrot's fine-tuned calculations, he would finally apprehend his antagonist, Scharlach. Although our detective, faithful to his fearless symmetries, had perhaps perceived a few subtle asymmetries lurking in the shadows, he nevertheless pushed them under the rug, opting to remain confident regarding his sleuthing capacities upon entering the house at the villa of Triste-le-Roy at the proper time where he had calculated that the crime was to take place. After pushing his way in [and] immediately sensing the "architect's preferences," he surmised that at the wall opposite to where he stood there would most likely be another stairway. And sure enough, there was. He ascended it, raised his hands, and opened a trap door. The house, however, soon thwarted his expectations. It was a labyrinth, but unlike ordinary labyrinths of two-dimensional maze-like qualities, it was three-dimensional. And to make matters worse, it was asymmetrical: it turned and twisted along vertical as well as horizontal pathways.

In the beginning it had all seemed so logical to Lönnrot, and things were going so well. The three murders plotted on a map of the city composed an equilateral triangle, and the murderer had declared that this, the final crime, had been committed. But Lönnrot was less than satisfied. Three is tension. In contrast, four is balance and harmony, the closest thing to perfect symmetry since breaking out of the sphere of unity and into the world of struggle, tears, and death. Lönnrot was convinced that a harmonious—albeit static—and timeless order was destined to triumph. Availing himself of the tools of his obstinate reason, he had calculated the day of the fourth crime, and with a compass he extrapolated the lines of the triangle on the map of the city before him to construct a rhombus: unwieldy one-dimensional lines stretched through an infinity of steps to join with one another, thus yielding two-dimensional order. Now, having entered the villa of Triste-le-Roy, Lönnrot's erstwhile intractable ideals are given a slap in the face by the befogging, bewildering reality confronting him. He is taken prisoner by Scharlach's henchmen, and suddenly discovers that he is to be his antagonist's fourth victim.

Before Scharlach kills Lönnrot, there is a brief verbal exchange during which time Scharlach explains how Lönnrot's ratiocination had been his undoing. Lönnrot, perhaps in a feeble attempt to prolong his demise, or perhaps as the ultimate exercise in ratiocination, proposes an alternative to Scharlach's labyrinth. "In your labyrinth there are three too many lines," he begins:

> I know of one Greek labyrinth which is a single straight line. Along that line so many philosophers have lost themselves that a mere detective might well do so, too. Scharlach, when in some

other incarnation you hunt me, pretend to commit (or do commit) a crime at A, then a second crime at B, eight kilometers from A, then a third crime at C, four kilometers from A and B, halfway between the two. Wait for me afterwards at D, two kilometers from A and C, again halfway between both. Kill me at D, as you are now going to kill me at Triste-le-Roy. (Borges 1962: 86-87)

Here, it is immediately apparent, we have Zeno and one of his paradoxes. There could be another murder at E, halfway between A and D, and another at F, halfway between A and E, and so on. And Lönnrot would never fall into Scharlach's trap. But he does. In this case, to continue from within Zeno's framework of logic, Scharlach could fire his pistol and the slug would first travel half way between A and B, to C, then halfway between C and B, to D, and so on: it would never reach its target.

But alas, Lönnrot surely errs once again. Scharlach's labyrinth is not of the conventional two-dimensional sort. It is three-dimensional, with implications of Scharlach's world within a four-dimensional space-time continuum which contains Lönnrot's helpless "worldline" within a three-dimensional space-time continuum. For Lönnrot, of course, the labyrinth Scharlach constructed is confusing, alienating, and maniacal. It is of the most *complex of complexities*, though for Scharlach it is quite *simple*. I hardly need write that in spite of his vague allusion to Zeno, Lönnrot could by no stretch of the imagination have prevented the bullet from reaching him. Scharlach's response to Lönnrot's proposal of a linear labyrinth reveals his confidence that Zeno is refuted in the practical affairs of everyday living: "The next time I kill you […] I promise you that labyrinth consisting of a single line which is invisible and unceasing" (Borges, 1962: 87). Granted, within Zeno's mighty logic, the slug from Scharlach's gun will never pierce Lönnrot's body. But, of course, that is another story, a story of intellection and ideation in some ethereal realm rather than of living and breathing within our concrete existence.

As it turned out, Lönnrot's scheme, developing linearly through time, was viewed from Scharlach's scheme *in toto*, as if he were in a higher, more complex, dimension looking upon Lönnrot's pitiful trajectory: it is much as if we were to observe, from above, a rat running what for us is a *simple* two-dimensional maze but for the rat it is of exceeding *complexity*. As a consequence, the symmetry of time as Lönnrot conceived it was of time in the strictly reversible sense within his three-dimensional world. Scharlach's conception, in contrast, was metaphorically speaking a dimension of time added to his own three-dimensions of space-roughly comparable to our own Einsteinian space-time continuum. Just as Lönnrot crept along his "world-line" within the equivalent of a two-dimensional spatial world, so also Scharlach, from whom Lönnrot's world is all there all at once as if on a plane, creeps along his own "world-line" within his own three-dimensional spatial world.

In other words, a rat running its maze traces a single irreversible line over a certain lapse of time in its effort to land its reward, but from our imperious three-dimensional vantage we can in one perceptual gulp see where it should and should not proceed. And after it has run the maze, we can see where it entered, where it went along its uncertain route, and how it came upon its reward. In comparable fashion, Lönnrot's construction of the mapped parallelogram from within Scharlach's world entailed first a replication of the triangle on his map pin-pointing the site of the first three homicides. Then Scharlach enacted the equivalent of a 180 flip in "three-dimensional" space such that the triangle's base lay adjacent to the base of its original triadic form. He had now located, from within another dimension, and timelessly so, the site of his next crime. This move contrasts with Lönnrot's time-bound rotation of the triangle on his two-dimensional plane, the map, as if he were within it and calculating the moves along a linear temporal trajectory. Scharlach's flip resting outside Lönnrot's field of vision, would be for Lönnrot, given his relatively helpless "two-dimensional" spatial perspective, a matter of seeing that the previous crime *was* there, and *now*, according to his calculations, the next crime *will be* there. There is a *past*, a knife-edge *now* racing through time, and a *future*. For Scharlach, in contrast, upon viewing Lönnrot's trajectory as if on a two-dimensional plane, there is simply a *before* and an *after*, in the sense of J. M. E. McTaggart's (1927) timeless B-series. Scharlach lives in time, to be sure, but his world consists of three spatial dimensions and one dimension of time. Lönnrot also lives in time. However, his map world, in contrast to that of Scharlach, consists essentially of two spatial dimensions and one of time, all of which is compacted into

Scharlach's three dimensions of space in an instant. Scharlach, then, is capable of seeing the whole of Lönnrot's trajectories in time in an instant.

>—Floyd Merrell, "Borges and Calvino: Chaosmos Unleashed," *Jorge Luis Borges: Thought and Knowledge in the XXth Century.* ed. Alfonso de Toro and Fernando de Toro, (Frankfurt: Vervuert, 1999): pp. 184-6.

PLOT SUMMARY OF
"Tlön, Uqbar, Orbis Tertius"

The story was first published in 1941 as part of the collection *El jardín de los senderos que se bifurcan* (*The Garden of Forking Paths*) and then reprinted in the larger volume *Ficciones* in 1944.

Quotes taken from Borges, Jorge Luis. *Ficciones*. intro. John Sturrock. (New York: Knopf, 1993): pp. 5-21. Alastair Reid translated the story.

With the often-quoted words—"I owe the discovery of Uqbar to the conjunction of a mirror and an encyclopedia" (6), Borges begins one of his most compelling tales. The mirror in question was at the end of a corridor. It reflected volumes of *The Anglo-American Cyclopedia*, which itself was a reproduction, that is, a reprint of the 1902 *Encyclopaedia Britannica*. As it turns out, Borges and Bioy Casares were talking at length after dining together. Ironically the topic of their conversation involved a writing project in which the first person narrator so altered the happenings in his tale such that only a few lucky readers would ever be able to fathom the banalities behind the text. While they talked, Borges felt that the mirror observed them. Bioy suddenly remembered that a heresiarch of Uqbar once stated "that mirrors and copulation are abominable, since they both multiply the numbers of man." (5) When Borges challenged him for the source of such a fact, Bioy cited the entry on Uqbar in *The Anglo-American Cyclopedia*. They consulted the volumes of the resource in vain for no matter what spelling of Uqbar they used, they found no such country mentioned.

The next day, Bioy phoned to say that he had the desired essay in his possession in Volume XLVI of said encyclopedia. In fact, he had misquoted the heresiarch who actually had condemned copulation and fatherhood. Some days later, Bioy brought the volume to the villa. He and Borges compared volumes. The only difference was an additional four pages that covered the article on Uqbar. They took care in reviewing the extra entry while noting a fundamental vagueness in its tone.

Details on the frontiers of Uqbar were exact but pointed to mountain ranges and rivers in the same unknown region. In the historical section, they learned that Uqbar had suffered religious persecution in the 13th century. Obelisks on the islands had survived this period. The portion on language and literature noted that all literature in Uqbar never referred to reality. A bibliography provided a list of resources that the two men were never able to find.

That same night they went to the National Library where it became clear to both of them that nobody had ever recorded being in Uqbar. Another colleague, Carlos Mastronardi, reported the next day that after coming across the same encyclopedia in a bookshop he had found no mention of Uqbar in Volume XLVI.

The second section of the story begins with reminiscences by the narrator about a certain engineer from the southern railroads by the name of Herbert Ashe. Tall and languid, Mr. Ashe had maintained what the narrator calls "one of those English friendships" with his father. That is to say they exchanged books and journals, they played chess—without speaking to one another—and generally avoided any intimacies. One afternoon in the Androgué hotel, Borges, and his father listened while Ashe discussed the duodecimal numerical system. Ashe commented that his current project involved converting duodecimal tables into sexagesimals for a Norwegian. Borges couldn't imagine anything more tedious or boring than Ashe and his projects.

In September 1937, some days before he died of an aneurysm, Ashe had received a package from Brazil, which contained a volume that Borges found months later in the bar of the hotel. When the narrator glanced at the book, he found that it was written in English, had 1001 pages, and was the 11th volume of *A First Encyclopedia of Tlön*. Two years had passed since his discovery of an encyclopedic entry on a false country and there before his eyes Borges read a fragment covering an unknown planet called Orbis Tertius. The volume covered:

> its architecture and its playing cards, its mythological terrors and the sound of its dialects, its emperors and its oceans, its minerals, its birds . . . all clearly stated, coherent, without any apparent dogmatic intention or parodic undertone. (9)

But the volume's discovery did not put to rest the mystery of Tlön. The entries referred to both preceding and subsequent volumes. This fact provoked scrutiny among known scholars who denied the existence of any other tomes. Another scholar, nevertheless, proposed that he and Borges's colleagues reconstruct the missing volumes. Alfonso Reyes calculated that one generation of Tlönists would be sufficient to accomplish this remarkable task. Borges took this proposal as cause for inquiring who might have been the first Tlönists. He assumed that there had been many, which would have required the participation of professionals from all fields to accomplish a "plan so vast that each individual contribution to it is infinitesimal." (10) Tlön had been considered chaos at first but the realization resulting from the volume's discovery was that a cosmos was at stake and that "the apparent contradictions in the eleventh volume are the basis for proving the existence of the others." (9)

It became clear that Tlön possessed an idealism in its realm in which its inhabitants partook in a diverse series of individual acts. The volume described an Ur language on Tlön that was devoid of nouns. Impersonal verbs were altered by monosyllabic suffixes or prefixes taking on the force of an adverb. In the southern hemisphere of Tlön, the monosyllabic adjective was preferred over the verb as the basic linguistic unit. Object descriptors were both visual and auditory. Other objects comprised multiple elements. Yet there was no limit to nouns in the language, though they did not refer to actual reality.

All professional disciplines in Tlön were inferior to psychology. Their idealism invalidated science, and to assign a name to something had the result of falsifying it. The metaphysicians of Tlön considered their profession a branch of fantastic literature. One school of metaphysics had reached the conclusion that time did not exist because the present was undefined, there was no reality in the future and the past was merely a present memory. Another school put forth that time had already happened and that life was a memory or reflection. A different group suggested that history was composed by the handwriting of a minor god communicating with a devil. One other school maintained that a symbol's meaning was true only every 300th night. Yet another theory held that while someone sleeps, he is awake somewhere else.

Despite these varying ideas of thought, the principle that provoked greatest debate was the Tlönist doctrine of materialism. To clarify the theory, an 11th century heresiarch recounted the parable of nine copper coins which X loses on Tuesday; four of which Y finds on Thursday rusted by Wednesday's rain; Z turns up three more on Friday, and X finds the remaining two the same day in his home. Did all nine coins, though lost, exist over the four days? The Tlönists debated the parable for a hundred years, until one thinker proposed: ". . . .there is only one Individual, and that this indivisible Individual is every one of the separate beings in the universe. . . X is Y and is Z. Z finds three coins because he remembers X lost them." (15) Finally, the 11th volume revealed that the Tlönist idealism succeeded because it rejected solipsism, it held psychology as the basis for all sciences, and it allowed a cult of gods to survive. In other matters, the volume explained that the geometry of Tlön was both visual and tactile. In literature, all works are the product of one timeless and anonymous author even though criticism tended to invent authors. One plot, altered in every possible variation, served for all books of fiction.

The force of idealism in Tlön revised reality such that objects once lost soon are duplicated. Much like the nine coins legend, the duplicates—known as *hrönir* on Tlön—result when ". . . [ ]Two people are looking for a pencil; the first one finds it and says nothing; the second finds a second pencil, no less real . . ." (16) Once the product of absent-mindedness, the *hrönir* had been produced for close to 100 years according to the 11th volume. A plan to fabricate *hrönir* was hatched at a state prison and soon spread to four colleges. One consequence of this scheme favored archeologists who, thanks to the *hrönir*, could then modify as well as question the past. Typically, though, objects that duplicate themselves could also eradicate their existence: "The classic example is that of a stone threshold which lasted as long as it was visited by a beggar, and which faded from sight on his death." (17) The narrator thus ends his essay in 1940.

The narrator's postscript dated 1947—longer than most appearing in Borges's stories—presents further proof of the infiltration of Tlön into the narrator's reality. Another chance discovery produces a letter in a volume owned by the deceased engineer Herbert Ashe. The letter, postmarked Ouro Preto, Brazil, revealed that Tlön was the invention of a 17th century secret society—Dalgarno and Berkeley among the membership. The society soon understood the need for disciples to carry on their work, and though persecuted, its membership reached as far as America in later years. In Memphis, Tennessee, around 1824, a society member recruited Ezra Buckley, a millionaire ascetic. Buckley's contribution to the project turned out to be significant. He favored the invention of an entire planet to be documented in an encyclopedia. Further, he would bequeath his fortune to fund the project provided the encyclopedia had "no truck with the imposter Jesus Christ." (18) In 1914, almost a century after Buckley's death, the society released the final volume to its 300 members. The 40 volumes comprising the encyclopedia, provisionally called Orbis Tertius, did not represent the end of the society's work. The members, among whom figured Ashe, planned another publication to be written in one of the languages of Tlön.

Around 1942, two more curious Tlönist events occurred. Among the contents of a delivery made to the Princess of Lucinge was a magnetic compass. Its markings matched those of an alphabet on Tlön. Then, the narrator and his friend Amorim sought shelter from a rising river at a general store. At dawn the next day, the man whose singing had disturbed everyone through the night was found dead. Among his possessions were coins and metal cones that turned out to be religious fetishes from Tlön.

Having discovered that Tlön was the invention of a secret society, the narrator felt compelled to face the fact that Tlön had penetrated his reality:

> Here I conclude the personal part of my narrative. The rest, when it is not in their hopes or their fears, is at least in the memories of all my readers. . . . A scattered dynasty of solitaries has changed the face of the world. Its task continues. If our foresight is not mistaken, a hundred years from now someone will discover the hundred volumes of the *Second Encyclopedia of Tlön*. (20, 21)

LIST OF CHARACTERS IN
"Tlön, Uqbar, Orbis Tertius"

Borges: An unnamed I recounts the fantastic tale that recreates the world of Tlön. The voice is that of Borges's persona as narrator, situated in Buenos Aires and accompanied by his frequent collaborator, Adolfo Bioy Casares.

Mirror: An inanimate protagonist in the story, it hung at the end of a hall and provoked a curious discovery.

The Anglo-American Cyclopedia: Another inanimate but vibrant participant, the text has several incarnations. In one, it exhibits an extra four pages representing the entry on Uqbar, a place that is equally shifty in its existence.

Bioy Casares: Here, in a textual reincarnation like the narrator, Bioy is the catalyst for pursuing the disturbing appearance and disappearance of encyclopedic entries. Bioy initially misquotes a saying from Uqbar and then steadfastly searches for textual evidence of the correct legend.

Carlos Mastronardi: Another friend in the narrator's circle of writing colleagues, Mastronardi comes upon another edition of *The Anglo-American Cyclopedia*, which lacks any mention of Uqbar.

Herbert Ashe: An English engineer and would-be mathematician, Ashe develops what the narrator terms a typical English friendship with the narrator's father. That is, they barely speak of intimacies if speak at all; they exchanges books, beat each other at chess without boasting, and generally but politely ignore each other socially. Shortly before his death, Ashe comes to possess volume 11 of *A First Encyclopedia of Tlön* that the narrator later discovers by chance.

Nestor Ibarra, Ezequiel Martínez Estrada, and Drieu La Rochelle: Colleagues and acquaintances of the narrator, they participate in the debate concerning the existence of other volumes belonging to *A First Encyclopedia of Tlön*.

Alfonso Reyes: A colleague of Bioy and the narrator, Reyes proposes that they unite to reconstruct the missing volumes of *A First Encyclopedia of Tlön.*

Xul Solar: Another of the narrator's cohorts, he translates a passage from one of the northern dialects of Tlön.

Ezra Buckley: An American tycoon in the early 1800s, Buckley suggests that the Tlönists expand their project from the invention of a country to that of a whole planet instead. Buckley promised to leave the society his fortune for this purpose as long as they did not mention Jesus in their writing. He was poisoned in Baton Rouge in 1828.

Princess of Faucigny Lucinge: One day in 1942, the princess received a crate of precious articles among which was a magnetic compass with markings originating from one of the alphabets of Tlön.

Amorim: A colleague of the narrator who purchases the coins and metal cones that a dead man leaves behind in a general store owned by a Brazilian. As it turns out, the objects were images of deities from Tlön.

CRITICAL VIEWS ON
"Tlön, Uqbar, Orbis Tertius"

DIDIER T. JAÉN ON ESOTERIC TRADITION

> [Professor Jaén has published several translations of poety as well as critical essays in journals such as *PMLA*, *Revista Iberoamericana*, *Hispania*, and others. Jaén defines the esoteric tradition as that collection of doctrines referring to "direct and secret knowledge of the origin of everything created." In this excerpt, Professor Jaén identifies the many philosophical allusions present in the second half of the story when the narrator discovers a complete volume of the *First Encyclopedia of Tlön*.]

In Part II of the story, the narrator discovers a complete volume of the *First Encyclopaedia* of *Tlön*. Tlön, we should remember, is one of the imaginary regions of the literature of Uqbar: "the literature of Uqbar is fantastic in character, and ... its epics and legends never referred to reality, but to the two imaginary regions of Mlenjas and Tlön" (19). If we identify Uqbar with the esoteric tradition, whose literature ("its epics and legends") is always allegorical and never refers to reality itself but to the realm of the spirit, or the Ideal, we can see the connection of Tlön with this literature, and the subtle reference to the relation of esoteric myth (the *Bhagavad Gita*, the *Avesta*, parts of Plato's *Republic*) with philosophical idealism. Not surprisingly then, the allusions related to the description of Tlön correspond, as has already been mentioned, to the development of philosophical idealism and its ramifications in modern sciences and philosophy from the seventeenth century to the present. From the point of view of our reading, just as Tlön is a product of Uqbar, philosophical idealism and certain branches of modern science would appear as products of the esoteric tradition, mainly Gnostic and Rosicrucian. Even in the answer the narrator gives to the question "who were the people who had invented Tlön?" (22) there is an indirect allusion to these origins:

> The plural is unavoidable, because we have unanimously rejected the idea of a single creator, some transcendental Leibniz working in modest obscurity. We conjecture that this "brave new world" was the work of a secret society of astronomers, biologists, engineers, metaphysicians, poets, chemists, mathematicians, moralists, painters and geometricians, all under the supervision of an unknown genius (22).

The allusion to Leibniz, presumably with reference to the variety and scope of his work, does not seem totally arbitrary in the context of our reading. Leibniz, occupied in his youth with the study of alchemical works during his stay in Nuremberg (towards 1667), was a member of a supposedly Rosicrucian society, although Leibniz himself, like Descartes, later publicly expressed doubts as to the real existence of such societies. On the other hand, the allusion to the "brave new world," although it suggests the work by Aldous Huxley (an important modern figure in esoteric studies), also takes us back to the seventeenth century, to Shakespeare's *The Tempest*, where the phrase originates (V:i, v. 181). The association of Prospero's island with the "New Atlantis" of Bacon, and of the latter with "The Land of the Rosicrucians" of John Heydon is a well known although discredited thesis. Finally, the apparently arbitrary list of professions enumerated by the narrator corresponds with the varied intellectual life of the seventeenth-century European Enlightenment (especially in England).

The description of the universe that is prevalent in Tlön begins with an allusion to Hume and to Berkeley. The latter's work, *Treatise Concerning the Principles of Human Knowledge*, published in 1710, establishes the basis of modern idealism. Hume carries Berkeley's premises to their logical consequences—to the negation of the reality of the subject, or of the personal self, a basic concept which Borges' literature shares with esoteric Gnostic and Buddhist doctrines. These points of view prevail in Tlön, and, after arguments characteristic of Borges himself, the logical process is carried to its final conclusion with the negation of the objective reality of time. Among the principles that support the negation of temporal reality, esoteric ideas of Gnostic and Buddhist origin are mixed with references to modern philosophers such as Bertrand Russell; all these are arguments that Borges himself uses in his essay "New Refutation of

Time." The result is a "monism, or extreme idealism [which] completely invalidates science" (24) and which makes of language, literature, and philosophy completely subjective operations.

>   —Didier T. Jaén, "The Esoteric Tradition in Borges' 'Tlön, Uqbar, Orbis Tertius'." *Studies in Short Fiction* 21 (Winter 1984): pp. 31-3.

EVELYN FISHBURN AND PSICHE HUGHES: DEFINITION OF ORBUS TERTIUS

> [While compiling their dictionary, the editors reported that they found themselves in a truly Borgesian universe since they were compelled to consult endless encyclopedias to trace all of Borges's allusions. Here they elaborate on the multi-lingual references found in the title of this story.]

Orbis Tertius
In 'Tlön, Uqbar, Orbis Tertius' the name given to a proposed encyclopaedia to be written in one of the languages of *Tlön, relating to an imaginary planet, or to what our planet will become under the influence of Tlön. The Latin name stands in marked contrast with the Nordic 'Tlön' and the Arabic 'Uqbar'. Explanation of it in terms of what we call the 'third world' seems unacceptably out of context; a more satisfying theory would be that it refers to a view in later *Gnosticism that an *orbis tertius* existed as an intermediary between the spiritual *orbis primus* and the inferior, or casual, *orbis alter*. The attempt to resolve the duality of *orbis primus* and *orbis alter* is reflected towards the end of the story of 'Tlön', where it is said that the penetration of our world with 'objects' from Tlön would eventually result in an 'Orbis Tertius'. Another explanation may be found in the Copernican heliocentric system, according to which Mercury and Venus are the first and second planets orbiting round the sun and Earth the third.
    Lab. 27 (3) *Ficc*. 13

>   — Evelyn Fishburn and Psiche Hughes, *A Dictionary of Borges*, (London: Duckworth, 1990): p. 177.

ROBERTO GONZÁLEZ ECHEVARRÍA ON THE STORY

[Roberto González Echevarría is Sterling Professor of Hispanic and Comparative Literatures. He is the author of numerous scholarly works including *The Voice of the Masters: Writing and Authority in Modern Latin American Literature* (1985) and *Celestina's Brood: Continuities of the Baroque in Spanish and Latin American Literatures* (1993), editor of *The Oxford Book of Latin American Short Stories* (1997) and coeditor of *The Cambridge History of Latin American Literature* (1996). His most recent publication is *The Pride of Havana: A History of Cuban Baseball* (1999). In this chapter, Professor González Echevarría closely examines the *novela de la tierra* (regionalist novel) and maintains that although Borges never wrote a novel he "offered a radical critique of anthropological discourse and its relationship to narrative." Here, González Echevarría points out that Borges uses an ethnographer's precision to create his imaginary country.]

In "Tlön, Uqbar, Orbis Tertius" Borges reveals the artifice of the regionalist novel by creating an entirely imaginary country described with the methodological precision of an ethnographer's report. In a sense, what Borges does is to turn the regionalist novel inside out, performing in the process a severe ideological critique of the anthropological mediation. The style of the entry in the encyclopedia, where the narrator finds the information, is described as follows: "El pasaje recordado por Bioy era tal vez el único sorprendente. El resto parecía muy verosímil, muy ajustado al tono general de la obra y (como es natural) un poco aburrido. Releyéndolo, descubrimos bajo su rigurosa escritura una fundamental vaguedad" (p. 432) ("The passage remembered by Bioy was perhaps the only startling one. The rest seemed probable enough, very much in keeping with the general tone of the work and, naturally, a little dull. Reading it over we discovered, beneath the rigorous writing, a fundamental vagueness" [p. 19]). The key word here is the technical term *verosímil*, lost in the somewhat careless translation, which means realistic by virtue of the text's adherence to rhetorical norms for representing reality. The suggestion is clear: regionalist novels are fantastic, not realistic, the methodology that legitimizes them is no more than a pre-text to elaborate a cogent fictional world. Ethnography is always literature. The authoritative voice of method is as literary, as fantastic, as the stories that it uncovers.

Borges had anticipated this critique in a 1932 essay that is a direct answer to an anthropological treatise that had vast repercussions in Latin American literature, as well as many others, James G. Frazer's *The Golden Bough*. In this essay, "El arte narrativo y la magia," Borges writes about novels and stories and their relation to the "primitive mind." He contends, as he will on several occasions, that novels are as chaotic as the real world, unless they are constructed like detective novels. Such stories, he says, are carefully constructed worlds in which there are secret connections between events. Borges is interested in the secret of those connections, which we accept without blinking. For Borges causality is the most important element in a story, but he asserts that causality in stories is as fantastic and as magical as the primitive cures described by Frazer, which depend on tropological relations between wound and cure, or between cure and and the weapon that inflicted the wound. Primitive medicine is based on belief in such a system of metaphors; magic would be the efficacy of such a system in affecting reality. In reading and writing stories, and in accepting detective stories as realistic, we indulge in the same kind of magic we assume to be typical of primitives. Hence our "study" of primitives by means of anthropology, and our writing about them using the literary conventions of ethnography, reveals much about us, much that is a mirror image of the object we purport to describe or analyze. The links that we establish between events, our own metatexts about the primitive, are cast in a rhetorical mold that is not radically unlike his. Given these propositions, Borges' Others in "Tlön, Uqbar, Orbis Tertius" are not going to be "contemporary savages," like those of Victorian anthropology, but imaginary beings that inhabit a kind of metatextual utopia.

In "Tlön, Uqbar, Orbis Tertius" that metatext happens to be about a non-existent realm, but the procedures and tropes that make it up are the same as those in ethnography; in fact, one could say that the story actualizes the metadiscourse of ethnography. The fable of validation or legitimation in Borges' story has, therefore, been internalized, has been made a part of the narrative. Legitimation is not granted here by a journey to the wild, by "being there," but by the discovery, in a pirated version of the *Britannica*, of an article about Uqbar, a country that the narrator and his friend Bioy cannot find in any atlas (Bioy is, of course, Adolfo Bioy Casares, an Argentine writer of fantastic fiction, a detail that vacuums into the fiction Borges' context at the time of writing). Uqbar is a very odd place indeed, but it is described by the encyclopedia, as we saw, in the flat tone characteristic of such reference works. A second fable of validation is provided by the appearance of another encyclopedia, produced by a character who is drawn out of the world of European expansion that generated modern anthropology. Legitimation in Borges does honor to the etymology of the word both as law and as reading. The textual space of the encyclopedia, which stands for all the knowledge in the West, a compendious and, at the same time, slightly frantic repository of information, is organized according to the most banal of conventions, the alphabet, yet can absorb anything, reducing to common knowledge the most distant and different cultural practices. Uqbar, knowledge of which the encyclopedia owes to the work of various German ethnographers and travelers, has a literature that is obsessively devoted to the description of two imaginary regions: Meljnas and Tlön. These are the telluric novels within the fictional telluric novel of Borges' story, the rest of which is about Tlön, one of those regions, which is as odd as Uqbar, if not more so. Information about Tlön is acquired from an *Encyclopedia of Tlön*, obtained from a blurry Englishman, appropriately named Herbert Ashe, who came to Argentina to work on the British-built railroads after some adventures in Brazil; he is obviously a figure of the European traveler, vaguely reminiscent of Francis Bond Head. Borges is notorious for the creation of this kind of *mise en abîme* to underline the textual nature of most phenomena. In this case, however, the presence of the encyclopedia in a remote neighborhood of Buenos Aires—as far as Borges would travel from the city—and the role played by the English engineer, clearly point not only to the literary nature of ethnographic writing, but also to the source of such discourse in institutions fostered by the British Empire. As we know, growth of the *Britannica* during the nineteenth century paralleled the expansion of the Empire, culminating in the tenth edition, published in 1902, the date given in Borges' story for the encyclopedia. Herbert Ashe merely heightens the atmosphere of Victorian colonial life that permeates "Tlön, Uqbar, Orbis Tertius."

> —Roberto González Echevarría, "The Novel as Myth and Archive: Ruins and Relics of Tlön," *Myth and Archive: A Theory of Latin American Narrative*, (Cambridge: Cambridge University Press, 1990): pp. 162-5.

BEATRIZ URRACA ON MIRRORS AND TLÖN

> [Beatriz Urraca has written critical studies on Sarmiento and Rafael Alberti. Professor Urraca also has published essays on traveling in Europe, Africa, and America in the mid-1800s. In her article, Professor Urraca examines mirror imaging and the technique of *mise en abime* as used by Borges in "Tlön, Uqbar, Orbis Tertius" and "La biblioteca de Babel" ("The Library of Babel"). In this excerpt, Urraca focuses on the totalities represented by the encyclopedia and the library as manifestations of human universes.]

The "mirror of words" that opens "Tlön, Uqbar, Orbis Tertius" acquires a new significance when we consider mirrors as a symbol for the human search for meaning. Borges's mirrors in the text are all of words, and words are our (imperfect) way of making sense of the world. This is the role of the figure of the encyclopedia, a "double" of the mirror as a textual *mise en abyme*. The encyclopedia is a work of language, and a reflection of the totality of the universe through words. Similarly, the story is an attempt to frame the infinite inside the mirror of its few pages. The encyclopedia is the organizing principle of the story, since Borges presents the data about Uqbar and Tlön according to the same divisions that we could find in any encyclopedia about our world, such as geography, history, language, literature, zoology, typography, philosophy, psychology, geometry . . . At the same time, as Eco suggests, there are other things to be found in an encyclopedia, and Borges's story, with its inclusion of all the possible philosophies and theories of the universe to be found in Tlön, does not fall short here either:

[The encyclopedia] does not register "truths" but, rather, what has been said about the truth or what has been believed to be true as well as what has been believed to be false or imaginary or legendary, provided that a given culture had elaborated some discourse about some subject matter. (Eco 83)

Like the encyclopedia, the Library is also a double of the mirror, for it contains books which are also made of words. (…)

If the encyclopedia can reflect a universe, the library can be one, for it contains all the books. Two of the most frequent motifs in Borges's works—the encyclopedia and the labyrinth—are used here as symbols of totality contained within a limited linguistic space, and they are the only earthly alternatives to the ultimate goal achieved by the poets of Tlön, who can transcend the limits of language and make a single word integrate an entire poetic object.

"Tlön, Uqbar, Orbis Tertius" and "La biblioteca de Babel" not only propose similar ideas and employ the same techniques, but also complement each other in a number of ways. From both of them the principle of duplication and multiplication emerges as one which links mirrors, men, and books as reflections of one another. The mirror in "Tlön, Uqbar, Orbis Tertius" suggests to Bioy Casares a sentence about mirrors and men found in an encyclopedia: "Los espejos y la cópula son abominables, porque multiplican el número de hombres" (T, 431). The mirror in the room is almost human, personified through verbs like "inquietaba," "acechaba;" in "La biblioteca" books are personified through the superstition of "el Hombre del Libro" (B, 469). In both stories, what we find is not a multiplication of men, but of books, for men can multiply the number of books as well as the number of men, and books are written having other books as pretext. In the first page there is The *Anglo-American Cyclopedia*, which is an imperfect reprint of *The Encyclopedia Britannica*. Only one copy of this *Anglo-American Cyclopedia* contains the article about Uqbar, because, according to the laws of the Library—which apply throughout the stories in *Ficciones*—"hay siempre varios centenares de miles de facsímiles imperfectos: de obras que no difieren sino por una letra o una coma" (B, 469). The article is finally found in a volume whose alphabetic notation does not include it; similarly, the Library contains a book whose cover does not prefigure what is inside. The forty-volume

First Encyclopedia of Tlön will be rewritten in one of the languages of Tlön as *Orbis Tertius*, and as *The Second Encyclopedia of Tlön*, which has not been found yet; finally, "Tlön, Uqbar, Orbis Tertius" stands as a story written about all these books.

—Beatriz Urraca, "Wor(l)ds Through the Looking-Glass: Borges's Mirrors and Contemporary Theory." *Revista Canadiense de Estudios Hispánicos* 17 (Otoño 1992) : pp. 162-3.

SYLVIA MOLLOY ON LANGUAGE

[Sylvia Molloy is the Albert Schweitzer Professor in the Humanities at New York University. Her work includes *La diffusion de la litérature hispano-américaine en France* (1972) and *At Face Value: Autobiographical Writing in Spanish America* (1990) along with many scholarly essays on Latin American literature and culture. In this translation of her *Las letras de Borges* (1979), Professor Molloy examines what she describes as "avoidance of fixity," an ongoing creation of allusions that Borges cautiously repeats and alters throughout his texts. In this excerpt, Professor Molloy concentrates on the language in "Tlön, Uqbar, Orbus Tertius" which, in her view, is used both to identify and to falsify.]

The conjectural language proposed by Borges in "Tlön, Uqbar, Orbis Tertius" assiduously avoids the substantive: it corresponds to a world that for its inhabitants, "is not a concourse of objects in space; it is a heterogeneous series of independent acts" (L 8). Language, or rather, languages in Tlön (since Borges proposes two ways of avoiding the name for the two hemispheres of that planet) appear as a linguistic flow that instead of stopping on the substantive intermittently stops on its modifiers. In Tlön the mere act of naming, of classifying, "implies a falsification" (L 10). The same thing happens with numbers. The mathematicians of Tlön maintain "that the operation of counting modifies quantities and converts them from indefinite into definite sums" (L 12). In Tlön there are neither names nor numbers; there is no *moon* because an effort is made to have no moon. Like *l'absente de tous bouquets*, it goes unnamed, alluded to and convoked by a divergence—a "transposition," as Mallarmé called it—that eludes direct naming. In Tlön's southern hemisphere one does not say "The moon rose above the river" but (with Joycean zeal) "upward behind the onstreaming it mooned" (L 8). In Tlön's northern hemisphere, the substantive is avoided through the accumulation of adjectives: again there is neither moon, nor moons, but "round airy-light on dark" or "pale-orange-of-the-sky" (L 9).

Borges writes of these new combinations that they are "ideal objects, which are convoked and dissolved in a moment, according to poetic needs" (L 9). Both these ways of avoiding the substantive recall Marcus Flaminius Rufus's fruitless pedagogical experiment in "The Immortal." The Roman tribune conceives of a plan to teach the troglodyte "to recognize and perhaps to repeat a few words": "I gave him the name Argos and tried to teach it to him. I failed over and again" (L 112). In view of his futile efforts to impose a rudimentary nomenclature on the other, and in order to account for his failure, the tribune resorts to an extravagant fancy, no different from the one on which the languages of Tlön are based:

> I thought that Argos and I participated in different universes; I thought that our perceptions were the same, but that he combined them in another way and made other objects of them; I thought that perhaps there were no objects for him, only a vertiginous and continuous play of extremely brief impressions. I thought of a world without memory, without time; I considered the possibility of a language without nouns, a language of impersonal verbs or indeclinable epithets. (L 112)

These poetic objects, whose elusive and transitory character is emphasized by Borges, signal a provisional halt within the flow of language, within the "vertiginous and continuous play" of writing; it is the provisional break made by the speaker, the scribe. On a linguistic level, these pauses recall Hermann Lotze's argument, as quoted by Borges, to elude the "multiplication of chimeras." Lotze "concludes that there is one single object in the world: an infinite and absolute substance, comparable to the God of Spinoza. The transferable causes are reduced to immanent ones; events, to manifestations or modalities of the cosmic substance" (OI 112). In the same way, one might say that in Tlön there is a single object, an infinite, absolute linguistic substance, obeying the same purpose: it avoids the substantive—the emblem *par excellence* of the chimera, of the rigid, paralyzing simulacrum—in order to stop sporadically on manifestations ("upward behind the onstreaming it mooned") or on modalities ("round airy-light on dark") of that substance itself; manifestations lasting the time of their utterance or of their inscription. However, Borges himself is the first to point out the flaws of this utopian proposition based on the rejection of the one and only name: "The fact that no one believes in the reality of nouns paradoxically causes their number to be unending. The languages of Tlön's northern hemisphere contain all the nouns of the Indo-European languages—and many others as well" (L 9). (…)

Duplicates in "Tlön, Uqbar, Orbis Tertius" have peculiar characteristics: they "are, though awkward in form, somewhat longer" (L 13). In sum, these "secondary objects" replicate an unnamed "original" and at the same time, diverge from it. Additionally, they are endowed with the power to question and modify, a power that Borges usually associates with the practice of literature. The methodical elaboration of these secondary objects or *hrönir*, in Tlön, "has made possible the interrogation and even the modification of the past, which is now no less plastic and docile than the future" (L 14).

—Sylvia Molloy, "Converting the Simulacrum," *Signs of Borges*, (Durham: Duke University Press, 1994): pp. 85-86, 87-8.

Gabriel Josipovici on Ideologies

[Author of *The Lessons of Modernism, and Other Essays* (1977) as well as several novels and short stories, Professor Josipovici borrows a line from Wallace Stevens—"the plain sense of things"—to highlight the absence of actuality in "Tlön, Uqbar, Orbus Tertius," which he believes conveys a sense of 'nowness'. In this excerpt, Josipovici points out the duplication implicit in the *hrönir* and the infiltration perpetrated by the secret society to suggest that Borges creates "a world overtaken by Nazi ideology."]

Centuries of idealism 'have not failed to influence reality', the narrator goes on, in a nice double negative. 'In the most ancient regions of Tlön, the duplication of lost objects is not infrequent.' Two persons look for a pencil; the first finds it and says nothing; the second finds a second pencil, 'no less real, but closer to his expectations' (*Labyrinths*, pp. 37-8). These secondary objects are called *hrönir*, and these *hrönir* have little by little been ousting the real, banal objects, so that the world of Tlön is approximating more and more to the expectations of its inhabitants.

The rest of the story tells how this fantastic world has slowly invaded our own, helped on by a secret society dedicated to Tlön and its propagation. This society, we are told, is 'benevolent', and included George Berkeley among its founder members. At first there were only isolated examples of infiltration, but these gradually turned into a trickle. By 1944 the trickle has become an avalanche: 'Manuals, anthologies, summaries, literal versions, authorised re-editions and pirated editions of the Greatest Work of Man flooded and still flood the earth. Almost immediately, reality yielded on more than one account. The truth is that it longed to yield. Ten years ago any symmetry with a semblance of order—dialectical materialism, anti-Semitism, Nazism—was sufficient to entrance the minds of men. How could one do other than submit to Tlön, to the minute and vast evidence of an orderly planet?' Our world, it seems, will soon be indistinguishable from Tlön: 'Already the schools have been invaded by the (conjectural) "primitive language" of Tlön; already the teaching of its harmonious history (filled with moving episodes) has wiped out the one which governed my childhood; already a fictitious past occupies in our memories the place of another, a past of which we know nothing with certainty—not even that it is false. . . . If our forecasts are not in error, a hundred years from now. . . English and French and mere Spanish will disappear from the globe. The world will be Tlön.'

At this point the narrator, who has not been much more that a literary device, suddenly takes centre stage: 'I pay no attention to all this', he writes, 'and go on revising, in the still days at the Adrogué hotel, an uncertain Quevedian translation (which I do not intend to publish) of Browne's *Urn Burial*' (*Labyrinths*, pp. 42-3).

It is easy enough to see the 'point' of the story: it is an anguished cry in the face of the persuasive ideologies which swept the world in the 1930s, and a kind of stoic refusal to submit to them. There is a puzzle about the dates: the story came out first in the collection *El jardín de senderos que se bifurcan* [The Garden of Forking Paths] in 1941, and was reprinted in the larger volume of 1944, *Ficciones* [Fictions]. Yet the latter part of the story is relegated to a postscript dated 1947. I presume this is a projection forward in time by the author writing in 1940 or 1941. He imagines then a world overtaken by Nazi ideology and dramatises what he would like his reaction to be: not so much passive resistance as a kind of quiet active resistance, the activity consisting of a completely selfless (he has no intention of publishing it) translation of a minor seventeenth-century prose work. The voluntary submission to a selfless task, to the carrying over into his native language of an author and a language far removed from him in space and intellectual interests, is the only way this quiet intellectual feels he can avoid being sucked into the idealist world of Tlön, that he can assert what he feels to be fundamental human values in a world rapidly turning into a mirror of our desires and imaginings.

It might be felt that the lumping together of 'dialectical materialism, anti-Semitism, Nazism' makes for a rather limp critique of the times, and that to see them all as one thing, and that thing an example of the idealist world of Tlön suggests a lack of political and historical acumen. Yet other stories—notably 'Deutsches Requiem'—as well as remarks he made in interviews, make it clear that the anglophile and democratic Borges was far from the uninvolved creator of private labyrinths he is often taken to be. On the other hand there is no doubt that the references to current events do seem rather perfunctory and that those stories, such as 'Deutsches Requiem', which deal with contemporary matters are not among his most successful. Indeed, one might say that they are among the least successful precisely because he assimilates a little too easily to his own concerns with the dangers of the imagination. It may be that Borges's mode of writing is not such as to engage fully with politics and history, like that of Sartre and Malraux: yet I would suggest that despite this his central contrast of the melancholy and resigned translator and the idealist world of Tlön is more deeply political than Malraux and Sartre can ever be, and that it helps to bring out something that is often overlooked in studies of literary modernism: that to write about politics without recognising the complicity of the forms of writing with the formation of political consciousness is to betray the cause one thinks one is serving, and that writers like Eliot, Stevens, Beckett and Borges may in the end be better guides to the times than Malraux, Sartre, Camus, Silone and the rest.

—Gabriel Josipovici, "Borges and the Plain Sense of Things," *Borges and Euorpe Revisited*. ed. Evelyn Fishburn. (London: University of London, 1998): pp. 61-2.

JORGE LUIS BORGES INTERVIEW ON TLÖN

[The extract comes from an interview conducted in English on November 21, 1969, in Madison, Wisconsin, by L. S. Dembo, author of critical works on Pound, Crane, and Nabokov. Here, Borges responds to Dembo's question regarding the recreation of the world in "Tlön, Uqbar, Orbis Tertius" and how it applies to a philosophy of idealism.]

Q. Anyway, let me continue with this question: One of your chief themes seems to be the ability of the mind to influence or recreate reality. I am thinking of the consummate recreation of the world in "Tlön, Uqbar, and Orbis Tertius." The philosophy of idealism prevalent on the imaginary planet Tlön seems to be vindicated when the actual world begins to transform itself in Tlön's image. Are you in fact a philosophic idealist or do you simply delight in paradoxes made possible by idealistic reasoning, or both?

A. Well, my father—I seem to be referring to him all the time; I greatly loved him, and I think of him as living—my father was a professor of psychology, and I remember—I was quite a small boy—when he began trying to teach me something of the puzzles that constitute the idealistic philosophy. And I remember once he explained to me, or he tried to explain to me, with the chessboard, the paradoxes of Xeno, Achilles and the Tortoise, and so on. I also remember that he held an orange in his hand and asked me, "Would you think of the taste of the orange as belonging to it?" And I said, "Well, I hardly know that. I suppose I'd have to taste the orange. I don't think the orange is tasting itself all the time." He replied, "That's quite a good answer," and then he went on to the color of the orange and asked, "Well, if you close your eyes, and if I put out the light, what color is the orange?" He didn't say a word about Berkeley or Hume, but he was really teaching me the philosophy of idealism, although, of course, he never used those words, because he thought they might scare me away. But he was teaching me a good many things, and he taught them as if they were of no importance at all. He was teaching me philosophy and psychology—that was his province—and he used William James as his textbook. He was teaching me all those things, and yet not allowing me to suspect that he was teaching me something.

Q. But you would say that you more or less were brought up on idealism?

A. Yes, and now when people tell me that they're down-to-earth and they tell me that I should be down-to-earth and think of reality, I wonder why a dream or an idea should be less real than this table for example, or why Macbeth should be less real than today's newspaper. I cannot quite understand this. I suppose if I had to define myself, I would define myself as an idealist, philosophically speaking. But I'm not sure I have to define myself. I'd rather go on wondering and puzzling about things, for I find that very enjoyable.

>—L. S. Dembo, "Jorge Luis Borges," *Jorge Luis Borges: Conversation*s, ed. Richard Burgin, (Jackson: University Press of Mississippi, 1998): pp. 85-6.

PLOT SUMMARY OF

"The Immortal"

Borges dedicated this tale to Cecilia Ingenieros when he first published it in his collection *El Aleph (The Aleph)* in 1949.

Quotes taken from Borges, Jorge Luis. *Collected Fictions.* trans. Andrew Hurley. (New York: Penguin, 1998): pp. 183-95.

The tale is laden with frames, layers, and voices. Borges, author, begins his story with an epithet from Francis Bacon quoting Solomon who said: "*There is no new thing upon the earth.*" (183) Then Borges, silent narrator, opens his tale in London in June of 1929. As it happens, the rare book dealer Joseph Cartaphilus has sold the six volumes of Pope's *Illiad* to the princess of Lucinge. It is her description of Cartaphilus that the narrator uses. She refers to the book dealer as an emaciated man with gray eyes and gray beard who speaks many languages but none very correctly. The princess hears later that Cartaphilus died at sea on his way home to Smyrna and was buried on the island of Ios. When she looks in the sixth volume of the *Illiad*, she finds the manuscript that is the central tale of this story. Borges as narrator assures the reader that the account, including its many Latinisms, is faithful to the document.

The manuscript recounts—in five parts—the travails of a tribune in a Roman legion at the time of the emperor Diocletian after leaving Thebes exhausted from wars in Egypt. His depression led him on an apparently impossible quest to find the City of the Immortals. He took up this pilgrimage because of the dying words of a bloody rider who arrived one night in the tribune's camp. The rider had come from "a mountain that lay beyond the Ganges" (184) and had traveled westward in search of a "river whose waters give immortality." (184)

The tribune became intrigued by these words. Some Mauritanian prisoners in the camp corroborated the dying man's account. In Rome, the tribune also consulted philosophers. He won the support of the Roman proconsul who provided the tribune with 200 soldiers for his quest. In addition, the tribune hired several mercenaries who falsely promised they knew the routes. As it turned out, the mercenaries were the first to desert the group while the soldiers fell to fever, death, insanity, and mutinies. The tribune found himself wandering alone in a desert where he fell into a deep dream about an orderly labyrinth in whose center the tribune would find a well with water to quench his thirst.

When the tribune awoke, he discovered that his hands were tied behind his back. In this second section of his manuscript, he found himself inside "an oblong stone niche no bigger than a common grave" (185) on the side of a mountain. Weakly, he raised his head, pounding with the pain of thirst, and saw the City of the Immortals at a distance. Near the fortifications on a stone plateau that made up the city, the tribune saw a group of naked men with gray skin and untended beards. He thought he recognized them as Troglodytes, mute men who eat serpents. Thirst drove him to throw himself down from the mountain niche. He fell into the water below, drank it like an animal, and fell again into a deep sleep.

An unknown number of days and nights passed. The Troglodytes neither helped nor hindered the tribune even when he begged them to kill him. When, after severing the bonds holding his hands and identifying himself as Marcus Flaminius Rufus, the proud legion succumbed to eating a serpent. Marcus Flaminius was then overcome by his desire to find the Immortals. His anxiety resulted in an inability to sleep. When he noticed that the Troglodytes didn't sleep either, he assumed they were keeping watch over him. At sunset, after praying out loud, Marcus Flaminius resolved to reach the city. At first, a few Troglodytes followed him. By midnight, he reached the city's walls and noticed that one Troglodyte had stayed with him on the long walk.

Weary and overwhelmed by the city's size, the tribune wandered around its perimeter until he finally took refuge inside a cavern. There he noticed a ladder rising from a pit. When he descended the ladder, Marcus Flaminius found himself in a round chamber. As he learned, eight of its nine doors led to a maze that brought him back to the same room. The ninth door opened to a second identical chamber. He wandered endlessly underground until a bright light dazzled him. Looking up to the source of the light, the tribune saw the blue sky and found that a stairway led up: "Thus it was that I was led to ascend from the blind realm of black and intertwining labyrinths into the brilliant city." (187)

Once above ground, Marcus Flaminius saw that he was in a courtyard surrounded by an irregularly shaped building of many different heights. The tremendous age of its construction stopped Marcus in his tracks as he sensed that the structure had existed since before mankind. Inside, the tribune wandered over the floors and up the staircases he found. As he walked, Marcus Flaminius thought that surely gods had constructed the building; then he believed that these gods must be dead. Finally, though, he told himself: "*The gods that built this place were mad.*" (188) The tribune's impressions of the palace were many and all disturbing: its great antiquity, its endlessness, its oppressiveness, and its irrationality—all led him to fear the City of the Immortals. The palace's maze showed Marcus Flaminius that it had no purpose. He began to doubt his own impressions and his transcription of the reality in front of him. The tribune sensed that he was caught in this same dream for many years. As he emerged from the City of Immortals, Marcus Flaminius realized that he remembered nothing else but his fear. He came to the conclusion that his loss of memory may have been willful.

In the third part of his manuscript, Marcus Flaminius turned his account to the one Troglodyte who silently followed him everywhere. The tribune became even more confused when he saw the Troglodyte draw and then erase a row of symbols in the sand: "The man would draw them, look at them, and correct them. Then suddenly, as though his game irritated him, he would rub them out with his palm and forearm." (189) It made no sense to Marcus Flaminius that a person, never learning to speak, would be able to write. Nevertheless, the tribune determined to teach the Troglodyte to speak.

Marcus Flaminius thought of a dog when observing the condition of the mute Troglodyte who followed him everywhere. Thus he gave the Troglodyte the name Argos, the same as Ulysses' old dog in the *Odyssey*. Though he tried repeatedly to teach Argos a few simple words, the tribune failed again and again. The Troglodyte's attitude bewildered the tribune. It was if a great distance separated them even though they were always together. Days turned into years when unexpectedly one morning a strong and most welcome rain began to fall. The tribune ran naked into the rain and called to Argos. As if the rain hadn't shocked the tribune, suddenly the Troglodyte quoted from the *Odyssey*: "This dog lying on the dungheap." (190) Despite his amazement, Marcus Flaminius asked Argos how much of the

Greek text he knew: "*Very little*, he replied. *Less than the meagerest rhapsode. It has been eleven hundred years since last I wrote it.*" (190)

The tribune recounts, in the fourth part of his manuscript, what he learned from Homer. The Troglodytes were the Immortals. Homer had been in the City of the Immortals a century when it was destroyed and it was on his counsel that they rebuilt the city on its own ruins. Homer revealed much to the tribune that day as he soon realized that the City's inhabitants knew nothing of death. Homer assured him, though, that the Immortals were not ascetics since thought brought them great and complex pleasure such that they preferred to spend their endless time in perfect quiet. Homer explained that no thing exists without being counterbalanced by another thing. So that if there is a river that bestows immortality, there must also be one that takes it away. Every act is the echo of another that preceded it in the past, without beginning and with no future. Homer and Marcus Flaminius separated in Tangiers without saying good-bye.

In the fifth and final part of his tale, the narrator reports that in the autumn of 1066 he fought at Stamford Bridge but could not remember for whom. Then, in a Samarkand prison, he recalled playing chess. He taught astrology in Bikanir and Bohemia. And in Aberdeen in 1714, he subscribed to the six volumes of Pope's *Illiad*. Some years later he discussed the same poem with a professor named Giambattista. Then again in 1921, he found himself on a ship that ran aground on the Eritrean coast. When leaving the ship, he remembered being a Roman tribune. It was then that the clear water in a spring attracted him. He scratched his hand against a thorny bush and in joy saw a drop of blood as he realized he was mortal once again.

As the narrator rereads the manuscript, he judges it to be false because he notes a joint authorship. He sees both Greek and Roman influences in its words and suspects the hand of Homer in the text. The narrator comes to understand that all memory disappears leaving only words. In a postscript from 1950, Borges the narrator comments on the intertextuality that the manuscript possesses. He offers a list of critical authorities who believe that, because of its many textual echoes, it is an apocryphal document and attribute the work to Joseph Cartaphilus, the rare book dealer. The narrator rejects their conclusion.

LIST OF CHARACTERS IN
"The Immortal"

Joseph Cartaphilus: The rare book dealer from Smyrna one day offered an edition of Pope's *Iliad* to the princess of Lucinge in his London shop. She described him as an emaciated and grimy man with gray eyes and beard. Cartaphilus spoke several languages fluently but not correctly. It was reported that he died at sea on his way home to Smyrna and was buried on the island of Ios.

The Princess of Lucinge: The princess is a purchaser of rare books who knows languages well enough to recognize the different dialects of Spanish and Portuguese that Cartaphilus uses. The princess also appears in another textual reincarnation in "Tlön, Uqbar, Orbus Tertius" as the Princess of Faucigny Lucinge.

Marcus Flaminius Rufus: The narrator of the tale from the found manuscript, he is tribune of a Roman legion in the time of the emperor Diocletian. Having been provoked by the zeal of a dying pilgrim, Marcus Flaminius picks up from where his journey ended to seek out the City of the Immortals. With 200 soldiers and several mercenaries, Marcus Flaminius leads an excursion into endless deserts. Alone after his men fall to sickness, death, desertions, and mutinies, he comes upon the Troglodytes outside the City of Immortals. Marcus Flaminius tries to teach one of them to speak. When the Troglodyte does talk, the tribune finds himself and his manuscript transformed.

Argos: This was the name of Ulysses' old dog in the *Odyssey*. Marcus Flaminius gives this name to the supposedly mute Troglodyte who follows him about the City of the Immortals much like a faithful dog would.

Homer: When Argos finally speaks, he recites a phrase from the *Odyssey*, the epic poem that he—Homer/Argos—wrote many hundreds of years earlier. A resident of the City of the Immortals, Homer lived there before it was destroyed and counseled that the city be rebuilt on its own ruins.

Narrator: The author of the postscript from 1950 is a first-person narrator who rejects the acceptability of others' conclusions regarding the found manuscript.

CRITICAL VIEWS ON
"The Immortal"

GEORGE R. MCMURRAY ON AN ALLEGORY OF THE
CREATIVE PROCESS

[Professor George McMurray has contributed significant critical studies on several Latin American authors including Gabriel García Márquez and José Donoso. Author of *Spanish American Writing Since 1941: A Critical Survey* (1987) and editor of *Critical Essays on Gabriel Garcia Marquez* (1987), McMurray believes that "El inmortal" ("The Immortal") is an allegory of the creative process. In this chapter of his book, Professor McMurray revisits the conditions in which Marcus Flaminius Rufus must work out a method of communication with Argos (Homer) and in doing so takes on a new identity when he becomes Homer.]

Marcus Flaminius Rufus is a man of action whose quest for eternal life frames the plot, but on a symbolic level he represents Cartaphilus's (Borges's) quest for literary immortality, which he will achieve through his identification with the immortal Homer. The process of this fusion of identities constitutes a crucial portion of the story. The chamber with nine doors that Rufus enters just prior to his arrival in the city represents the womb from which he will emerge as a would-be man of letters, the nine doors symbolizing the nine-month gestation period. The "mad" City of the Immortals evokes a vision of the chaotic world he wishes to organize and depict. The reason for his initial failure becomes evident when, immediately after fleeing the city, he attempts to communicate with Argos and discovers the defects of language and thought (note the ironic use of anaphora in the following quotation), his only tools for creating his work of art. As he explains, "I thought that Argos and I participated in different universes; I thought that our perceptions were the same, but that he combined them in another way and made other objects of them; I thought that perhaps there were no objects for him, only a vertiginous and continuous play of extremely brief impressions. I thought of a world without memory, without time; I considered the possibility of a language without nouns, a language of impersonal verbs or indeclinable epithets."

The long-awaited rain that facilitates communication between Rufus and Argos (Homer) symbolizes inspiration and perhaps intuition, elements far more useful to the creative artist than thought. Through inspiration, then, Rufus assumes the identity of Homer and, as one of the Immortals, reveals to the reader the "laws" of this strange realm. His assertions that "a single immortal is all men" and "no one is anyone" suggest the story's pantheistic theme, elucidated by the plot, that one author is all authors. The Immortals' concept of time as a series of recurring events is expressed metaphorically when the narrator reappears under new identities but in archetypal situations similar to those of either Rufus or Homer. Thus he relives Rufus's military career when he fights at Stamford Bridge in 1066 and becomes Homer again when he transcribes the adventures of Sinbad and rediscovers the *Iliad*. The last of the narrator's identities, which, we suspect, represents Cartaphilus himself, is that of a traveler on his way to Bombay in 1921, when he regains mortality. Eight years later Cartaphilus dies. The final words of his manuscript, written shortly before his death, convey the temporal anguish of an author who knows he has achieved immortality in his writings but, nevertheless, faces the disintegration of his mortal self: "When the end draws near, there no longer remain any remembered images; only words remain …. I have been Homer; shortly, I shall be No One, like Ulysses; shortly, I shall be all men; I shall be dead."

—George R. McMurray, "Borges and the Absurd Human Condition." *Jorge Luis Borges*. (New York: Frederick Ungar Publishing Co., 1980): pp: 84-5.

Michael Evans on Intertextuality

[Author of *Basic Grammar for Medieval and Renaissance Studies* (1995) and critical essays on Machiavelli and intertextualism, Professor Evans views this tale as a circular one constructed from endless textual permutations. Evans maintains, in this excerpt, that Borges does not incorporate the many intertextual allusions merely to challenge the reader. Rather, Evans concludes in this essay, Borges uses the many fictional labyrinths to support his vision of philosophical Idealism.]

It would be misguided, however, to infer from these intertextual relations that Borges's story is concerned with challenging the reader to trace the origin of the various quotations and thereby to indulge in some vast literary game of detection. Although a non-intertextual reading of "El Inmortal" would be incomplete and fragmentary, the reader is nevertheless not primarily directed to turn to the works of De Quincey, Pliny, Virgil, Homer and the other authors. Indeed the main object of the narrative (and one which is underscored by the chorus of intertextual intrusions) is to convey a sense of the indeterminate and the infinite. Instead of naming them "allusions," the postscript more aptly refers to the intertextual elements in "El Inmortal" as "intrusions," and one could add that as intrusions they invade the text and fracture it into a mosaic of separate but echoing parts. The two most conspicuous instances of intertextual intrusion are dramatically emphasised by being spoken "into" the text through the passive medium of the unwitting characters. The first is the line from Homer's *Iliad*, II, 824 ("los ricos teucros de Zelea que beben el agua negra del Esepo" ["Those from Zeleia wealthy Trojans, who drink the water of dark Aisepos... (186)]) and the second is from the *Odyssey* XVII,394 ("Este perro tirado en el estiércol" ["This dog lying on the dungheap" (190)]). The former quotation is spoken "inexplicablemente" and uncontrollably by Rufus as he drinks from the river of immortality, and the latter quotation is uttered by Argos/Homer bathing in the downpour of rain mentioned earlier. The intrusive nature of the lines is heightened by the fact that they are not formulated by the characters but transmitted through them. Mere vehicles for mouthing the extraneous words, the characters have become points of intersection between the texts of Homer and Borges.

—Michael Evans, "Intertextual Labyrinth: 'El inmortal' by Borges." *Forum for Modern Language Studies*. 20 (July 1984): pp. 277-8.

EVELYN FISHBURN AND PSICHE HUGHES: DEFINITION OF
JOSEPH CARTAPHILUS

[Evelyn Fishburn is the author of *The Portrayal of Immigration in Nineteenth Century Argentine Fiction (1845-1902)* [1981] and the editor of *Borges and Europe Revisited* (1998). Psiche Hughes has published critical essays on Manuel Puig and Alejo Carpentier as well as studies of women writers in Latin American literature. The dictionary began as a project after consulting with Borges and receiving his encouragement. In this entry, the editors explain the connection between the character Cartaphilus and the legend of the Wandering Jew.]

Cartaphilus, Joseph
A fictional character in 'The Immortal'. His name alludes to the legend of the Wandering Jew, which first appeared in a thirteenth-century chronicle by Roger Wendover. According to Wendover, a certain Cartaphilus (believed to be St Joseph of Arimathaea), taunted Jesus on his way to the Cross and was told by him that he would have to wait on earth until he returned. Cartaphilus lived to a hundred and then reverted to thirty, at which age he was destined to remain until the end of the world. Lab. 135 (105): the legend of the Jew condemned to wander about the world until Christ's second coming has been told in several versions and was a popular subject in the eighteenth and nineteenth centuries. Through these reworkings the legend shares with the *Odyssey the fate of '*immortality*' (see 'Las versiones homéricas' in *Disc.*).
   Lab. 135 (105) *Aleph* 7

>—Evelyn Fishburn and Psiche Hughes, *A Dictionary of Borges*. (London: Duckworth, 1990): p. 50.

EVELYN FISHBURN AND PSICHE HUGHES: DEFINITION OF
ARGOS

[Fishburn and Hughes researched the many allusions used by Borges in his short stories to assist the reader with the numerous intertextual echoes present in the text. According to the creators of this helpful resource, the legion's naming of the Troglodyte as Argos, like other such references in Borges's work, is not "gratuitous or merely ornamental."]

'Argos…This dog lying in the manure' ('Este perro tirado en el estiércol')
In the '*Odyssey* Odysseus' faithful dog, who is the first to recognise him on his return to Ithaca. Lab. 143 (113): the passage describes how Odysseus had raised and trained the dog but never hunted with him before leaving for the Trojan war. Nineteen years later Argos is lying 'on the deep pile of dung' which is to be used for manure: 'Now, as he perceived that Odysseus had come close to him, / he wagged his tail, and laid back both his ears…' and died (*Odyssey* 17. 290-327).
Lab. 142/3 (112/13) *Aleph* 17/8

—Evelyn Fishburn and Psiche Hughes. *A Dictionary of Borge*s. (London: Duckworth, 1990): p. 19-20.

JON STEWART ON CHRISTIAN VIEW OF IMMORTALITY

[Jon Stewart has published several critical essays on Borges covering *El libro de arena* (*Book of Sand*), "Funes el memorioso," and the concepts of language and translation in Borges's work. Professor Stewart argues here that Borges intends to criticize both Greek and Christian views of immortality in his story. In this excerpt, Stewart concludes that Borges's criticism refers, at least once, to Christian doctrine. The problem as Stewart sees it is how to reconcile the positive view Christianity has of immortality with the meaningless and undesirable picture that Borges implies in his version of unending life.]

Although Borges's story seems at face value to be a criticism solely of the Greeks' conception of immortality, since after all it is the Olympian gods that the tribune finds in such a base state, nevertheless Borges clearly intends for this criticism also to be valid for the Christian view. He refers directly to the Christian doctrine once (p. 144), but in addition to this direct reference, there are other subtler bits of evidence that single out specifically the Christian doctrine of immortality. The state of the immortals is described as one of "pure speculation" (p. 144), which is precisely the description of the *visio beatifica* given by Augustine and Aquinas, in which one contemplates God and the workings of the universe for all eternity. The immortals are described as being so lost in the realm of thought that they gradually lose touch with the mundane: "Absorbed in thought, they hardly perceived the physical world" (p. 144). This accords with Aquinas's analysis that in the *visio beatifica* we behold only *divina substantia*. The blessed perceive the universe only in terms of divine substance and thus do not see the physical world or mundane substance *per se*. The blessed state of the immortals is also alluded to when the tribune observes that "the Immortals were capable of perfect quietude" (p. 145). This then echoes the claim of Aquinas that in the *visio beatifica* we will enjoy perfect bliss as well as Augustine's claim that we will be perfectly at leisure. The tribune, having become immortal, explains how the greatest pleasure was pure thought: "There is no pleasure more complex than that of thought and we surrendered ourselves to it" (p. 145). Here we see the claim of Augustine and Aquinas that pure speculation in the *visio beatifica* is the greatest bliss that man can experience.

The problem that "The Immortal" presents is how to reconcile the optimistic account of immortality that Christianity offers with the fact, which Borges so poignantly illustrates, that such a life of immortality would be meaningless, bovine, and undesirable. Not accidently the *visio beatifica* reduces the life of immortality to a troglodyte condition insofar as it precludes meaningful activity by removing obstacles and by introducing an infinite time frame. The sort of difficulties and challenges that render our mundane existence meaningful are precisely what makes heaven appear at first glance attractive. If, indeed, it is true that at the termination of our mundane existence, we will become immortal, then as Borges shows, we will not become holy saints living blissfully in heaven beholding God and the universe for an eternity but rather base and indifferent troglodytes eating lizards and tracing inchoate figures in the sands of unknown deserts.

—Jon Stewart, "Borges on Immortality." *Philosophy and Literature*. 17 (October 1993): pp. 300-1.

Harold Bloom on the Irony Present in the Story

> [Bloom maintains that Borges's use of irony in the story about the Roman tribune's quest enhances the nightmarish tone of the tale. In this excerpt, Professor Bloom states that the story produces "an anguish of contamination" reducing even Homer to the commonplace.]

"The Immortal" could be entitled "Homer and the Labyrinth," since those two entities, the author and the ruined, labyrinthine City of the Immortals, constitute the story. Rufus the tribune, who goes on a quest to find the City of the Immortals, sees his double in the rather frightening figure who turns out to be Homer, first of the immortal poets. Ronald J. Christ (a Borgesian name!) in *The Narrow Act: Borges' Art of Illusion* reads the story as a Conradian-Eliotic journey to the symbolic Heart of Darkness. The analogue is useful if we discount the moral element in Conrad, which finds no place in "The Immortal" and is only rarely central in Borges, whose greatness is allied to his heroic aestheticism, which repudiates conventional moral and societal concerns and even plays ironically at devaluing Homer, as though his epic art was commonplace.

Homer, like Shakespeare, is for Borges the Maker or archetypal poet, but also the archetypal man, like Blake's Albion or Joyce's Earwicker (Here Comes Everyone), which must be why Borges, with whatever irony, could describe "The Immortal" as the "outline of an ethic for immortals." This ethic turns out to be only Borges' customary evasion of the family romance of literature, his idealization of influence relationships. All writers are equal; originality is unlikely. Homer and Shakespeare, being everyone and anyone, render individuality impossible, so personality is an out-moded myth. We all live forever, so there will be time to read everyone and everything, as there is in Shaw's *Back to Methuselah,* one of the prime sources of "The Immortal."

This literary idealism, if it were not laced with savage irony, would render Borges insipid and make "The Immortal" a kind of parody-prophecy of a multiculturalist manifesto. No need to fear: the story is Borges' bleakest and most chilling nightmare, and the idealization of literature is reduced by Swiftian irony to a nihilistic pessimism, in which immortality is seen as the greatest nightmare of all, a dream architecture that can only be labyrinthine. Of all Borges' phantasmagorias, the City of the Immortals is the most dismaying. Rufus the tribune, exploring it, finds it to be "so horrible that its mere existence ... contaminates the past and the future and in some way even jeopardizes the stars."

The crucial word there is "contaminates," and the dominant affect of "The Immortal" is an anguish of contamination. Homer, when he first identifies himself, is a mute, wretched, snake-eating troglodyte, and the much sought River of Immortality is only a sandy rivulet. Like the other Immortals, Homer has been all but destroyed by a life of "pure speculation." If Hamlet indeed thought not too much but too wisely, then Borges' Homer (who is also Shakespeare) has thought not too well, but too endlessly. Partly Borges is satirizing *Back to Methuselah*, but he is also savaging his own literary idealism. Without rivalry and polemic between the Immortals there is, paradoxically, no life, and literature dies. For Borges, all theology is a division of fantastic literature. In "The Immortal" he observes with superb irony that despite their professed belief in immortality, Jews, Christians, and Moslems venerate only this world because they truly believe only in it and bind future states to it only as rewards or punishments.

—Harold Bloom, "Borges, Neruda, and Pessoa: Hispanic-Portugues Whitman." *The Western Canon: The Books and School of the Ages.* (New York: Harcourt Brace & Company, 1994): pp: 472-4.

DOMINIQUE JULLIEN ON BIOGRAPHIES OF AN IMMORTAL

[The author of *Proust et ses modeles: les Mille et une nuits et les Memoires* (1989) and *Recits du nouveau monde: les voyageurs français en Amérique de Chateaubriand a nos jours* (1992), Professor Jullien has also published many critical essays on Stendhal and Diderot as well as about the work of Borges. In the present article, Professor Jullien compares two Borges stories—"El hacedor" and "El inmortal"—to examine how Borges constructs a biography of immortal figures. In this excerpt, Jullien calls attention to the elements of the Wandering Jew legend at play in the text.]

(...) Borges's Immortal doubles as the Wandering Jew. The story is, like the myth, built on the amalgamation of diverse cultural elements. By conflating the Roman soldier and the antiquarian, the story mirrors the initial contamination (a Roman, Cartaphilus, and a Jew, Ahasuerus) which gave rise to the legend of the Wandering Jew. The Immortal is likewise a composite of several mythical wanderers and storytellers. Cartaphilus's many travels and aliases make him an avatar of Ulysses and Sinbad the Sailor, who also find their way into the story, since Cartaphilus recounts having copied, "en el siglo trece, las aventuras de Simbad, de otro Ulises" (*Obras* 1:543). Homer and the Immortal, Ulysses the Greek and Sinbad the Arab, the tribune of imperial Rome and the Wandering Jew all come together in a text that makes them one universal wanderer.

In Borges's version, the Christian lesson conveyed by the legend (the wandering as divine punishment) is left out. What interests Borges is solely the question of identity, which holds the potential for both the fantastic and the allegorical dimensions. He picks up a mythical figure that, as a result of gradual universalization, has become a form without a content; his version of the legend turns the Wandering Jew from a symbol of all humankind into an impersonal author of all literature.

Like its protagonist, the legend is cosmopolitan and ubiquitous. The same story is told in many languages and versions; the same character appears under several aliases: Joseph Cartaphilus, Isaac Laquedem, Ahasuerus, Giovanni Buttadeus, Juan de Espera en Dios, et cetera. Multiple identities also define (or rather blur) the portrait of the Immortal; cosmopolitanism characterizes his autobiography, translated into Spanish from an original written in English (Borges's favorite literary language) but filled with Latinisms. The choice of English and of the name Cartaphilus (instead of the more common Ahasuerus) suggests that the legend was given its first written form in England: it is appropriate that an island people should be attracted by the story of an endless journey. This is highlighted in De Quincey's writings (one of the "intrusions and thefts" discovered by Dr. Cordovero in his *Coat of many Colours*). The Everlasting Jew,

De Quincey writes, "is the German name for what we English call the Wandering Jew. The German imagination has been most struck by the duration of the man's life, and his unhappy sanctity from death: the English by the unrestingness of the man's life, his incapacity of repose."

The cosmopolitan nature of the legend, combined with the universality of the wandering motif, is what makes "El inmortal" a sort of compendium of Borgesian themes.

—Dominique Jullien, "Biography of an Immortal." *Comparative Literature.* 47 (Spring 1995): pp. 138-9.

RENÉ DE COSTA ON HUMOR IN BORGES

[Professor in the Department of Romance Languages & Literatures at the University of Chicago, René de Costa has published extensively on numerous topics in Latin American literature. His works include *Poetry of Pablo Neruda* (1979), *Vicente Huidobro: The Careers of a Poet* (1984) as well as a critical edition of *Los herarldos negros* by Cesar Vallejo (1998). In the present work, Professor de Costa studies the work of Borges to discover how he makes the serious funny. This excerpt considers "El inmortal" ("The Immortal"): one of Borges's "most seemingly serious stories." Here, Professor de Costa examines the false solemnity of the narrator's voice and how it changes—when mixed with Latinisms—throughout the tale.]

The central narrative, purportedly the literal translation into Spanish of an English-language manuscript consisting of five numbered chapterlike sequences, is framed by an introductory paragraph in a serious authoritative voice with a characteristically false solemnity, a voice to be sure just like that of Borges, reporting in detail on how the document came into his hands. We are told that the presumed author of the manuscript is a London antique dealer, from whom the reporter's friend, the "Princess of Lucinge" (another real-life personality: an Argentine heiress impoverished after her marriage to a penniless European "aristocrat," a friend whom Borges had cited for a similar cameo role in the anachronical postscript to "Tlön"), purchased the first edition of Alexander Pope's verse translation of Homer's *Iliad* (1720). The manuscript, "written in English and plagued with Latinisms," was found by the "Princess" in the last volume of the set. The bookdealer's name is Joseph Cartaphilus, not coincidentally one of the names of the "Wandering Jew." *Britannica*'s entry on this figure is typically to the point: "a character doomed to live until the end of the world because he taunted Jesus on the way to the Crucifixion."(…)

It is in chapter 5, reading over what he has written, "in English, with abundant Latinisms," that our twentieth-century manuscript penman finds that something is gravely wrong. Borges has him observe with appropriate new critical acumen, that although the account seems to have been written by a soldier, "el narrador no repara en lo bélico y sí en la suerte de los hombres" [the narrator does not deal with the incidents of war but with the fates of men]. His judgment is that the story seems "unreal" because it mixes together the events of many "different men," from Homer to Joseph Cartaphilus. Echoing the Chinaman's jibe at the "remote" British Empire in "The Garden of Forking Paths," Borges has the twentieth-century-bookman-turned-literary-critic find it bizarre that Homer, reincarnated as Pope, "descubra, a la vuelta de muchos siglos, en un *reino boreal*, y un idioma bárbaro, las formas de su Ilíada" [should discover, after so many centuries, in a *northern kingdom* and a barbarous tongue, the forms of his Iliad]. A parable-like illustration of the "eternal return," of the endless repetition of historical cycles as witnessed by one man who is all men, "an immortal, who precisely because he is immortal, forgets his past" (as told to Charbonnier in *Entretiens avec Jorge Luis Borges* [1967]).

Not a small part of what makes this story amusing derives from the skillful flow of its changing narrative voice, a voice that provides the reader with just enough information to see through and beyond the character-protagonists in each stage of their journey through time, to see through their time-framed eyes far more than they can see. This is the other side of irony, and in this way we come to regard them as comic figures, unaware of their limitations. The reader, knowing more about them than they themselves do, can smile at their incongruities. We know that the haughty tribune is a coward, we know that he awakens to immortality in a paleo-Christian cemetery, we know that his troglodytes are Vandals, we know the historical outcome of the various battles that he flees from, we know that the barbarian, having forgotten Greek, is Homer, and that the antique dealer from Smyrna is the Wandering Jew; we know, in sum, much more than the characters know about themselves in any of their many incarnations. And this superior knowledge, ironically provided to us through them and by them, is what permits us to laugh at their nescience. Laughter provides us with epiphanies, sudden illuminations regarding the thrust of the story, which is indeed about the plight of what things might be like on the treadmill of immortality.

—René de Costa, "*Fun in Fictions* and *The Aleph.*" *Humor in Borges.* (Detroit: Wayne State University Press, 2000): pp. 87-88, 90-91.

PLOT SUMMARY OF

"The Aleph"

Borges published "El Aleph" in 1945 and dedicated the story to Estela Canto.

Quotations from "The Aleph" in Borges, Jorge Luis. *The Aleph and Other Stories: 1933-1969.* ed. and trans. Norman Thomas di Giovanni. (New York: E. P. Dutton & Co., Inc., 1970): pp. 15-30.

The death of Beatriz Viterbo in February of 1929 clearly saddens the narrator. As he walks through the city, he is reminded by his surroundings that the universe has changed and will continue changing after her death. The narrator is reassured, nevertheless, that he now can "devote myself to her memory . . . without humiliation" (15) as Beatriz can no longer become annoyed by his devotion to her. The narrator begins yearly visits on her birthday, April 30, to her home on Garay Street where her cousin, Carlos Argentino Daneri, and her father live. The visits allow the narrator the chance to review her many photographs and to be in space she once occupied. His visits are punctual and short at first, arriving the first year at 7:15 and staying for 25 minutes. With each year, however, his arrival time slips and he manages to stay longer "on these melancholy and vainly erotic anniversaries." (16) By 1941, the narrator has come into the confidence of cousin Carlos and is regularly invited to stay to dinner.

The narrator remarks that the conversational subjects Daneri discusses are entirely meaningless and full of pointless analogies. One evening in particular, while Daneri expounds on the glorification of modern man, the narrator asks him if Daneri has ever considered writing about his theories and opinions. As it turns out, Daneri has spent many years secretly doing exactly that. His project is a massive poem to describe the entire planet entitled *The Earth,* the poem of which covers his thoughts on man. After reading a passage from the poem at the narrator's request, Daneri proceeds to analyze the beauty of his own work that, in his opinion, appeals to the academic as well as the Hellenist, includes allusions to the Baroque, and offers bilingual phrases and a novel rhyme scheme. The narrator finds himself forced to listen to many other stanzas that he quietly judges to be both extravagant and deadly dull. He discovers that Daneri has finished sections covering all of Australia and many parts of Argentina. But Daneri confessed "only the fear of creating an army of implacable and powerful enemies dissuaded him . . . from fearlessly publishing this poem." (19, note)

Two weeks later, Daneri invited the narrator to a cocktail party at a salon-bar owned by Zunino and Zungri, his landlords. The poet read more fragments of his opus and explained to the narrator how he had revised several passages by using "azures, ceruleans, and ultramarines" (20) instead of the more common "blue." And although he condemned the practice of having prefaces in modern books, Daneri admitted that one might serve as an attention-getter for his work. The narrator feared that he would be enlisted for such a task; instead, Daneri requested that the narrator approach Alvaro Melián Lafinur for this purpose at the next meeting of the Writer's Club. At once relieved but adverse to speaking to Alvaro on Daneri's behalf, the narrator decided not to mention it.

Some time had passed when, convinced that Daneri had forgotten his request, the narrator received a telephone call from a very disturbed Daneri. His "ancestral home" was about to be demolished by his landlords. The narrator momentarily shared his distress by first recognizing that at a certain age any change becomes more difficult and then associating the house to be destroyed with Beatriz. The real problem though, as Daneri revealed, was that it would be impossible for him to finish his great poem without the Aleph—"one of the points in space that contains all other points." (23) He explained:
'It's in the cellar under the dining room', he went on, so overcome by his worries now that he forgot to be pompous. 'It's mine—mine. I discovered it when I was a child, all by myself'. (23)

According to Daneri, possession of the Aleph was his inalienable right and he would contract the services of a lawyer to sue the landlords for damages. It was at this point that the narrator questioned why he had never suspected that Carlos Argentino was mad.

The narrator quickly went to the house on Garay Street. While waiting for Daneri, he mumbled to the photographs of Beatriz on the piano and identified himself: "Beatriz, Beatriz Elena, Beatriz Elena Viterbo, darling Beatriz, Beatriz now gone forever, it's me, it's Borges." (24) Daneri entered, observed the narrator, and then escorted him to the spot in the basement where he should lay prone in the dark and concentrate on the 19th step in the staircase. When Daneri left the narrator in the pitch-black darkness and closed the cellar door, panic set in. The narrator now feared that a madman had locked him in a cellar. In his dread, he closed his eyes. When he next opened them, he saw the Aleph and explained: "What my eyes beheld was simultaneous, but what I now write down will be successive, because language is successive." (26) The narrator described "the teeming sea," "the multitudes of America," "all the mirrors on earth." His list of wonders continued:

> I saw all the ants on the planet; I saw a Persian astrolabe; I saw in the drawer of a writing table (and the handwriting made me tremble) unbelievable, obscene, detailed letters, which Beatriz had written to Carlos Argentino . . . I saw my own face and my own bowels; I saw your face; and I felt dizzy and wept. . . (27-8)

His reverie was interrupted by Daneri's voice coming to him out of the darkness as he declared that the narrator could never possibly pay him back for such a marvelous revelation. It was then that Borges discovered his revenge against Daneri. He refused to discuss the Aleph, recommended a quiet country retreat to Daneri, and left the house. After a few sleepless nights, he returned to the regularity of oblivious life.

In a postscript from March 1943, the narrator notes that some six months after the demolition of the house on Garay Street, the publishing house of Procrustes & Co. released a printing of the section of Daneri's opus covering the Argentine sections. For this, Daneri received the Second National Prize for Literature, while the narrator's recent publication garnered no award. He closed his note by observing that the Aleph is the first letter of the Hebrew alphabet meaning, in Kabbalist tradition, "pure and boundless godhead." (29) Regardless of the origin of its name and past events, the narrator had arrived at the conclusion that the Aleph in the basement of Daneri's house was a false one. He based this theory on a manuscript in which Captain Burton, the British Consul in Brazil in the 1860s, describes five famous mirrors around the globe. Burton's manuscript further states that the entire universe can be found inside a stone pillar in the Amr mosque in Cairo. The narrator closes his tale wondering whether the true Aleph exists inside that stone pillar or whether like the image of Beatriz it fades in his porous and forgetful mind.

LIST OF CHARACTERS IN

"The Aleph"

Beatriz Viterbo: The object of affection for both her cousin Daneri and the narrator. Beatriz' death in February 1929 marks the beginning of yearly visits to her home on the anniversary of her birthday. Beatriz, described as tall and frail, was once married to Roberto Alessandri, had a Pekinese lapdog, and was captured forever in many photos and in the narrator's memory.

Borges: The first person narrator commemorates Beatriz' life by his visits to her father and cousin. At first these are short visits, but as the years go by, the narrator finds ways to arrive later and stay longer. It is because of these visits that the narrator and Daneri form a peculiar relationship in which the narrator, a writer by profession, learns of Daneri's lifelong project and a mysterious object in the basement of his house.

Carlos Argentino Daneri: A pink-faced and overweight but delicately featured man, Daneri, though a third-generation Italian, speaks with characteristic Italian pronunciation and gestures. The narrator describes his conversations as continuous and meaningless, both pointless and trivial. Daneri believes that man through the connectivity that science and technology offer will find travel in the future to be superfluous. His lifelong project consists of writing a poem in hexameters entitled *The Earth*, which by 1941 includes stanzas covering all of Australia and parts of Argentina along with many personal digressions.

Zunino and Zungri: Daneri's landlords offer a party at a local salon-bar to which Daneri invites the narrator. When the landlords decide to demolish his house, however, Daneri reacts hysterically and explains to the narrator that the mystery in his basement must be protected at all cost for without it Daneri will never be able to finish his poem.

Alvaro Melián Lafinur: A colleague of the narrator who belongs to the Writer's Club. Daneri hopes that Alvaro will graciously write an introduction to his poem.

Doctor Zunni: This is Daneri's lawyer who is expected to sue the landlords, Zunino and Zungri, for damages at the mere mention of demolishing the house.

Procrustes & Co.: In a postscript, the narrator reveals that this publishing house has printed—with considerable success—a first section of Daneri's poem covering Argentina and plans to publish a second segment.

Captain Burton: British Consul in Brazil around 1867, Burton wrote a manuscript on five famous mirrors. From this manuscript the narrator concludes that although the Aleph may indeed exist, as Burton suggests inside a stone pillar at the Amr mosque in Cairo, that the one in Daneri's basement is a false Aleph.

CRITICAL VIEWS ON
"The Aleph"

Jorge Luis Borges Writing About "The Aleph"

[A mischievous Borges first tells of an encounter with an ingenuous journalist in Buenos Aires and then explains the challenge he faced when writing "El Aleph" ("The Aleph"). Borges also identifies the story's main protagonists: Beatriz Viterbo and Carlos Argentino Daneri.]

Once, in Madrid, a journalist asked me whether Buenos Aires actually possessed an Aleph. I nearly yielded to temptation and said yes, but a friend broke in and pointed out that were such an object to exist it would not only be the most famous thing in the world but would renew our whole conception of time, astronomy, mathematics, and space. "Ah," said the journalist, "so the entire thing is your invention. I thought it was true because you gave the name of the street." I did not dare tell him that the naming of streets is not much of a feat.

My chief problem in writing the story lay in what Walt Whitman had very successfully achieved—the setting down of a limited catalog of endless things. The task, as is evident, is impossible, for such chaotic enumeration can only be simulated, and every apparently haphazard element has to be linked to its neighbor either by secret association or by contrast.

"The Aleph" has been praised by readers for its variety of elements: the fantastic, the satiric, the autobiographical, and the pathetic. I wonder whether our modern worship of complexity is not wrong, however. I wonder whether a short story should be so ambitious. Critics, going even further, have detected Beatrice Portinari in Beatriz Viterbo, Dante in Daneri, and the descent into hell in the descent into the cellar. I am, of course, duly grateful for these unlooked-for gifts.

Beatriz Viterbo really existed and I was very much and hopelessly in love with her. I wrote my story after her death. Carlos Argentino Daneri is a friend of mine, still living, who to this day has never suspected he is in the story. The verses are a parody of his verse. Daneri's speech on the other hand is not an exaggeration but a fair rendering. The Argentine Academy of Letters is the habitat of such specimens.

>—Jorge Luis Borges. *The Aleph and Other Stories: 1933-1969.* Norman Thomas di Giovanni, ed. and trans. (New York: E. P. Dutton Co., Inc., 1970): p. 264.

JON THIEM ON BORGES-DANTE PARALLELS

[Professor Thiem has published many critical essays on topics including the translator, the reader, and the library. In 1991, his edition and translation *Lorenzo de Medici, Poems and Prose* was printed by the Pennsylvania State University Press. In the present essay, Professor Thiem outlines a "theme of total enumeration" and a "method of significant omission" that characterize Borges's story and its echoes of Dante. This excerpt shows the parallels between "El Aleph" ("The Aleph") and Dante's *Paradiso*.]

Of the numerous parallels between Dante's work and "The Aleph" the most significant for an interpretation of the poetics of Borges's story relate to the *Paradiso*. These in particular have been convincingly established in separate studies by Alberto Carlos, Roberto Paoli (44-45) and Ruggiero Stefanini. Foremost is the striking similarity beween Dante's God in the *Paradiso* and the Aleph, Borges's total point. Borges the narrator sees the Aleph as "a tiny iridescent sphere of almost intolerable brilliance," "una pequena esfera tornasolada, de casi intolerable fulgor (167). Similarly, Dante the pilgrim sees God as a mere point of light which nevertheless makes the eye want to close because of its piercing brilliance (28.13-21). Just as Beatrice describes God as "that place where every *ubi* and every *quando* is centered in a point." "là ve s'appunta ogne *ubi* e ogne *quandro*" (29.12), so too the Aleph is "one of the points in space that contains all the [other] points," "uno de los puntos del espacio que contienen todos los puntos" (160). The pilgrim in his final vision of the divine point of light sees confined in its depths "all that lies scattered in pages throughout the universe," "ciò che per l'universo si squaderna" (33.87). Likewise Borges sees in the Aleph the whole "unimaginable universe," "el inconcebible universo" (166). More important still, each work presents a spatial paradox that also involves a perceptual anomaly: not just a point that is all points, but a point in which all other points remain discernible to the human eye ("El Aleph" 161, 164; *Paradiso* 30.118-123, 31.19-24). Each work, in short, concerns itself with the nature and scope of total vision.

Other parallels suggest that Borges uses the *Paradiso* to set up a poetics of total vision, in other words a study of the principles and limits of expressing a total vision by means of verbal art. The first canto of the *Paradiso* states the well-known problem: "through words it is not possible to signify transhuman matters," "Transhumanar significar *per verba*/non se poria" (70-71). Throughout the *Paradiso* Dante regrets his inability to remember or put into language his visionary experiences. These regrets reach a crescendo in the last canto where he repeatedly laments that the ultimate vision he has received exceeds a human's verbal and mnemonic capacities to set it forth (55-57, 82-84, 94-96, 106-108, 133-136), and he likens the evanescence of his vision to the "unsealing" of snow by the sun and to the scattering by the wind of the light leaves of the Sibyl so that the "meaning," "sentenza," of her oracle is lost (64-66). His difficulty lies not only in the magnitude or totality of the vision, but also in its remarkable concentration, for, as he says, he sees "confined, / bound by love into a single volume, / all that lies scattered in pages throughout the universe," "s'interna, / legato conamore in un volume, / ciò che per l'universo si squaderna" (85-87). Thus, though the pilgrim sees all-in-one, the poet cannot describe all-in-one by human means, except scatter-fashion, as a sort of sequence in which the all ceases to be all, and the one becomes several, presented in succession.

—Jon Thiem, "Borges, Dante, and the Poetics of Total Vision." *Comparative Literature* 40 (Spring 1988): pp. 100-2.

EVELYN FISHBURN AND PSICHE HUGHES: DEFINITION OF ALEPH

[The Kabbalistic definition of Aleph, as noted here by the editors of this beneficial dictionary, provides the reader with an initial guide for understanding what can be viewed under the 19th stair in the basement of Daneri's house.]

Aleph
The first letter of the Hebrew alphabet, with a numerical value of one. Aleph 11 (15): though silent and used mainly to indicate vowel punctuation, the aleph in *Cabbalistic belief is considered the foremost Hebrew letter, a symbol of all the other letters and thus, by extension, of the universe itself. One of the many interpretations of the Aleph is that its symmetrical shape symbolises the concept that everything in the lower world is a reflection of its archetypal form in the world above. In mathematics it indicates a higher power of infinity than integer numbers or numbers that are on a straight line. This allows for the concept of a plurality of alephs, or infinities. See *Cabbala, *Mengenlehre.

Lab. 55 (30) *Ficc.* 67, Aleph 11 (15) *Aleph* 151

—Evelyn Fishburn and Psiche Hughes. *A Dictionary of Borges.* (London: Duckworth, 1990): p. 9.

María Rosa Menocal on Visions of Beatriz/Beatrice

[Professor Menocal is the R. Seldon Rose Professor of Spanish at Yale University. She is the author of *The Arabic Role in Medieval Literary History* (1987) and *Shards of Love: Exile and the Origins of the Lyric* (1994), coeditor of *The Literature of Al-Andalus* from Cambridge University Press (2000), as well as numerous scholarly studies on medieval texts and Rock music. This excerpt from her chapter "Blindness: Alephs and Lovers" cites Thiem's thesis on the presence of Dante in "El Aleph" ("The Aleph") and offers a counter-argument based on Beatriz/Beatrice as envisioned by Borges and a 'Petrarchan' Dante.]

Borges's Beatriz, especially in conjunction with his essays on Beatrice in the *Purgatorio and Paradiso*, is a fulcrum of images and meanings, the stark emblem of why pity and sadness and disappointments haunt all those pages; and it is through her that we sense most clearly those great misgivings Borges has about Dante. For the pity exists not because she is dead but because the author never knew how to recover her, even in death, and because her cruelty, her absences, finally made him turn away. It should be clear from the necessarily fragmented recounting of "The Aleph" I have given that there is a cacophony of poetic voices in the story—and that they are attached to more than one character: the Dante created here is as much the Borges as the Daneri. (In great measure, of course, this is what prevents its being a simple parody.) For Dante as Daneri, Beatriz is a necessary but unspoken attachment, a cousin whose pictures are still scattered throughout his house, and he is a man who welcomes a stranger to his house to commemorate her birthday, years after her death. But her name never passes his lips—it is never even clear he understood what that Borges was doing in his house every thirtieth of April—and it is eventually evident that his great attachment is, of course, the Aleph, his inspiration, his source, his magic touchstone.

At first Daneri himself has no importance for Borges except as the cousin to the dead Beatriz—a Beatriz, one is compelled to note, who is never described as alive except at the instant Borges comes to the conclusion that Daneri is mad, and decides that she probably was as well.

> Beatriz (yo mismo suelo repetirlo) era una mujer, una niña, de una clarividencia casi implacable, pero había en ella negligencias, distracciones, desdenes, verdaderas crueldades, que tal vez reclamaban una explicación patológica.

> Beatriz (I myself often say it) was a woman, a child, with almost uncanny powers of clairvoyance, but forgetfulness, distractions, contempt, and a streak of cruelty were also in her, and perhaps these called for a pathological explanation.

The beloved, then, was infinitely unworthy, that same Beatrice who is created cruel even in the *Purgatorio* and *Paradiso*. And then, slowly, Daneri becomes much more, and Borges's remaining attachments to her are merely incantational, like the habit of a prayer, and a vulgar one at that. Daneri, finally, is the link not to his cousin but to the Aleph itself, and thus, for Borges, Beatriz herself is but the first step to the grand vision, to that moment of clairvoyance and ineffability in the basement of her ancestral home. This, in the end, was all she really gave him, although it would seem it was perhaps a great deal, because she appears to have been otherwise unable to be fulfilling at all. Borges, like Petrarch, is a stunning and magical historian and in a handful of lines can lay bare the ambition and the hurt—each in their own way part of the obsession with truth—that are two sides of the same coin:

> Carlos Argentina observó, con admiración rencorosa, que no creía errar en el epiteto al calificar de sólido el prestigio logrado en todos los círculos por Alvaro Melián Lafinur, hombre de letras... yo tenía que hacerme portavoz de dos méritos inconclusos: la perfección formal y el rigor científico, "porque ese dilatado jardín de tropos, de figuras, de galanuras, no tolera un solo detalle que no confirme la severa verdad." Agregó que Beatriz siempre se había distraído con Alvaro.

> Carlos Argentino [Daneri] remarked, with admiration and envy, that surely he could not be far wrong in qualifying with the epithet "solid" the prestige enjoyed in every circle by Alvaro Melián Lafinur, a man of letters . . . he [Daneri] suggested I make myself spokesman for two of the book's undeniable virtues—formal perfection and scientific rigor—"inasmuch as this wide garden of metaphors, of figures of speech, of elegances, is inhospitable to the least detail not strictly upholding of truth." He added that Beatriz had always been taken with Alvaro.

Hurt and ambition. Little wonder, given such a reading of the *Vita nuova* and the *Commedia*, that Borges prefaces his remarks to the encounter with Beatrice in the *Paradiso* with that arresting "I want to comment on the most moving [literally, full of pathos] verses literature has ever produced." But there is more than even that, implicitly, that is pathetic, pitiable, for Borges the writer and the consumer and inventor of writers is not so irreducibly romantic that even the most irremediable of romantic attachments would in and of itself provoke such great pathos in him. Clearly, it is the result, at least in this case, as he sees it, of that failure in love: the abandonment of even the possibility of love poetry for the Aleph in the basement, for that clairvoyance, that universal and epic vision. For the sight of what others might call empire, or grandeur, or God.

> Se Virgilio et Omero avessin visto
> quel sole il qual vegg'io con gli occhi miei,
> tutte lor forze in dar fama a costei
> avrian posto et l'un stil coll'altro misto;
>
> di che sarebbe Enea turbato, et tristo
> Achille, Ulisse et gli altri semidei,
> et quel che resse anni cinquantasei
> si bene il mondo, et quel ch'ancise Egisto....

If Virgil and Homer had seen that sun which I see with my eyes, they would have exerted all their powers to give her fame and would have mixed together the two styles:

For which Aeneas would be angry; and Achilles, Ulysses, and the other demigods, and he who ruled the world so well for fifty-six years, and he whom Aegisthus killed, would all be sad.... (Petrarch, *Rime sparse*, Poem 186, first two stanzas of sonnet)

> —María Rosa Menocal, "Blindness: Alephs and Lovers." *Writing in Dante's Cult of Truth: From Borges to Boccaccio.* (Durham: Duke University Press, 1991): pp. 160-3.

JORGE LUIS BORGES ON THE STORY

> [Selden Rodman, author of poetic analyses and many travelogues covering South America, recounts here a conversation with Borges in which Rodman distinctly feels that Borges is joking. Rodman later asks about the destruction of the house in "El Aleph" ("The Aleph").]

I told Borges that I was haunted by his story "El Aleph," especially by the passage describing the magical appearance on the cellar step of the small iridescent sphere "whose center is everywhere and its circumference no-where." I asked him about the connection between the first part of the story and the last. "It's not clear to me." And I explained why.

"Now that you mention it, it's not clear to me either," he said. "I think I'll change it and put in a much clearer relation between the buyer of the house and the seller, a hint at the very beginning that someone is going to buy the house. And I will put your name in it too, if you have no objection, as a tribute to you for improving it."

I laughed. Was he pulling my leg, mildly making fun of me—which he had every right to do? He told me about a reporter in Madrid who had come to him and asked him seriously whether the Aleph existed in fact. "Later on I wished I had encouraged him in this tomfoolery, but at the time I said, 'Of course not,' and he left quite crestfallen, and even disgusted with me for making such a deception! Tomfoolery should always be encouraged, don't you agree? But I let the poor man down and he felt disconsolate." He added that the poet satirized at the beginning of the story was drawn from life and that his mother had begged him not to make it so obvious. "But I said to her: 'He'll never recognize himself'—and he didn't!" I asked him where he found the title. "I took it from Bertrand Russell's Introduction to his *Philosophy of Mathematics*, where it is used as the symbol for transfinite numbers."

"Why is the house in which the Aleph appears destroyed in the end?" I asked.

"It had to be destroyed," he said, "because you can't leave things like an Aleph lying around in this day and age, the way Aladdin left his lamp lying around. Not any more. The premises have to be tidied up, the supernatural suitably disposed of, the reader's mind set at rest."

—Selden Rodman *Jorge Luis Borges: Conversations.* ed. Richard Burgin, (Jackson: University Press of Mississippi, 1998): pp. 102-3.

NADA ELIA ON ISLAMIC MYSTICISM IN THE STORY

[The author of *Trances, Dances, and Vociferations: Agency and Resistance in Africana Women's Narrative* (2001), Professor Elia has also written on post-colonial narrative as well as Algerian and Maghrebi literature. In this excerpt, Elia examines "El Aleph" ("The Aleph") and another short story, "El zahir" ("The Zahir") for their similar threads of Islamic mysticism. Her point of departure involves not only common elements—the death of a beloved, Buenos Aires as locale, and obsessions—but also contrasting Arabic terms *zahir* meaning visible or apparent and its antonym—*batin* (inner, concealed).]

"Belief in the Zahir is of Islamic origin," wrote Borges, the narrator in Jorge Luis Borges's short story "The Zahir" (200). This narrator is not absolutely sure who he is, nor what has happened to him, but he is sure something has happened to him, which has changed the course of his life. He has come across the Zahir. Borges, the narrator of "The Aleph," is at a loss for words: "And here begins my despair as a writer. All language is a set of symbols whose use among its speakers assumes a shared past" (160). But his experience is unique, and therefore uncommunicable. For he has seen the Aleph.

"The Zahir" and "The Aleph," although written a number of years apart, are frequently paired by critics, as a number of stylistic and thematic parallels invite the comparison. The narrator in both stories is a man, Borges, who has had an experience that proves to be a revelation. This experience, in both cases, has left an indelible trace on him, left him a different person. In both cases, he finds himself questioning his sanity and unable to express what he has seen. In both cases, he becomes obsessed with his vision. Even minor, textual details correspond in the two stories: both begin with the death of a beloved woman and take place in Buenos Aires, as distinct from some abstract "universal" locale. The spiritual affinity, however, spans further back in time and space. (. . .)

The Aleph is not as material, as obvious a manifestation of Allah, hence the person who sees it must be closer to selflessness, to a total immersion into God's creation, to a loss of all that is proper to his/her individuality. "I saw all the mirrors on earth, and none of them reflected me" ("Aleph" 161), Borges recalls, thus suggesting that, at least while his vision lasted, his individual existence was uncertain. Immediately after this vision of "the inconceivable universe," Borges manages to "pick [him]self up and utter: 'One hell of a–yes, one hell of a–' The matter-of-factedness of my voice surprised me" (162).

Borges the narrator and Carlos Argentino, in "The Aleph," were rivals, competing for Beatriz's attention. A *zahiri* reading of this passage would therefore refer to a reluctance on Borges' part to admit

Carlos Argentino's clear advantage, for the latter is Beatriz' cousin, and the Aleph was seen under his own roof. A *batini* reading is much richer: Borges, having experienced a direct vision, grows indifferent to Beatriz, the mediator, the guide (who, moreover, was not sufficiently qualified to guide the visionary Dante through Paradiso, but abandoned him instead at the outer gates of Purgatorio). Borges' voice, his medium of expression and communication, becomes "matter of fact." But Borges and Carlos Argentino are also two writers competing for the same literary prize, which the latter wins, because Borges could not put, in "successive language," his vision of the universe. In this instance too, Borges is indifferent to Carlos Argentino's material, worldly, and wordly success, and to his own failure.

—Nada Elia, "Islamic Esoteric Concepts as Borges Strategies." *Variaciones Borges* 5 (1998): pp. 130-1, 136-7.

María Kodama on Mystical Experience

[Amanuensis and wife, María Kodama de Borges worked and lived with Borges in the final years of his life and shared the aesthetics with which Borges guided his life. Kodama collaborated with Borges on his *Breve antologia anglosajona* (1978) and *Atlas* (1984). In this article, Kodama considers the relation between Borges and religion. She notes the diverse religious background that Borges's family represented: a Catholic mother and an English grandmother who recited verses from the Bible. In this excerpt, Kodama considers the Hindu figure Atmán in relation to "El Aleph" ("The Aleph") since this god is "totally independent from the coordinates of time and space."]

(. . .) We know that the mystical experiences cannot be communicated, that they do not last for a long time, although those devoted to an ascetic life are able to repeat such experiences with a certain frequency. When experiencing a mystical state, the subject passively receives something, an awareness of being endowed with a different power, something that is different to everything that is known or felt in that moment: the being fuses himself with a different universe, out of time and space, where everything falls into place. This pure consciousness, incorporated to the whole, has little to do with the everyday Subject, which is subjected to changes and deterioration.

For the Hindus, this I of which we are aware is not real: there is another one which is the real one: the Atmán, which for some is not the real, but for other is such that it is: the Atmán is totally independent from the coordinates of time and space. All this reminds us of Schopenhauer's characterization of the Pure Subject of knowledge, for whom the creation or contemplation of works of arts constitutes a mode of salvation, the access to Nirvana, where will-power vanishes while the aesthetic emotion that fuses the Subject and Object lasts. We only have to think about "El Simurgh y el Águila," a story in *Nueve ensayos dantescos*, where Borges narrates a passage that was read to him in his childhood. Farid the Din Attar was the author of the strange Simurgh (Thirty birds). He was a Persian who belonged to the Sufi sect; he had a drugstore, and one afternoon he was visited by a Muslim Monk who told him that it will be most difficult for him to abandon his riches. Attar abandoned his store and became a pilgrim. He traveled to strange places and then he arrived at Meca. In his return to his motherland, he wrote poems and devoted himself to contemplation. Among his works we find *El coloquio de los pájaros* (*Mantiq-al-Tayr*). Near his death, he stopped writing. In the *Mantiq-al-Tayr*, the king of the birds, the Simurgh drops a feather in China. All the birds decide to find their king. They know that his name means "Thirty birds" and that his dwelling is in a circular mountain which surrounds the Earth. After overcoming a series of obstacles they arrived at their king's home and they discover that the Semurgh is each one and all of them. Here, again, we have the pantheistic idea of the One as the only reality. The Sufi counted among their people great mystic poets, and this is why Borges, an ardent reader of oriental philosophies and religions, could not but be most interested. (. . .)

Again, in "El Aleph" (1989: 617–628), the narrator will go through the experience where the writer becomes desperate in his attempt to capture words, knowing beforehand that his attempt is futile, since nothing will give him or communicate to him, to that instrument of fables, the writer of chains and signs, the vision of the infinite, of the simultaneity that escapes the imposed succession, :

[. . .] vi en el Aleph la tierra y en la tierra otra vez el Aleph y en el Aleph la tierra, vi mi cara y mis vísceras, vi tu cara, y sentí vértigo y lloré, porque mis ojos habían visto ese objeto secreto y conjectural, cuyo nombre usurpan los hombres, pero que ningún hombre ha mirado: el inconcebible universo. (ibid: 626)

Typically, the mystical experience also bursts in here in an unexpected manner, in a place discovered by a mediocre writer (the basement where the narrator goes), and it is experienced by a sceptic who has only agreed to contemplate the Aleph in order to please the host. But the moment of illumination lived does change the narrator, who will return stripped of his individuality, to the petty and small world which he confronts with Carlos Argentino Daneri. Perhaps because a deliberate practice of an aesthetic period or a total surrendering to his art did not take place, the narrator does not suffer changes which could mark him in a definite way. Of this experience he only keeps an intellectual knowledge, but not the indescribable emotion which totally changes the I of Tzinacán.

The narrator of "El Aleph" is a witness, an incredible observer of the unknowable university; Tzinacán achieves the union with the divinity; Borges, the great reader, often imagined the Paradise as being an infinite library.

—María Kodama de Borges, "Jorge Luis Borges, Religions and the Mystical Experience." *Jorge Luis Borges: Thought and Knowledge in the XXth Century.* ed. Alfonso de Toro and Fernando de Toro. (Frankfurt: Vervuert, 1999): pp. 22-3, 24.

PLOT SUMMARY OF

"The South"

This story appeared as "El sur" in the collection *Ficciones* in 1944.

Quotes taken from Borges, Jorge Luis. *Ficciones*. intro. John Sturrock. (New York: Knopf, 1993): pp. 135-42. Anthony Kerrigan translated the story.

Juan Dahlmann takes pride in the very Argentine heritage represented by his maternal grandfather Francisco Flores more so than in his paternal grandfather, Johannes Dahlmann, an Evangelical minister who arrived in Buenos Aires in 1871. Dahlmann is so fiercely but quietly nationalistic that he conserves a sword from Flores, his daguerreotype, and the family farm, described by the narrator as "the empty shell of a ranch in the South." (135) Dahlmann's work kept him in Buenos Aires but each summer he was sustained by the idea that the ranch awaited him. Suddenly, however, in February 1939, Dahlmann's ordered world changed.

On the same afternoon that Dahlmann acquired Weil's edition of *The Thousand and One Nights*, he hurried up to his flat to examine it. As he ascended the stairs, something seemed to brush by his head. Only when he saw the horrified look on his neighbor's face did Dahlmann realize that he had blood on his forehead. The wound provoked a severe fever. More than a week passed while friends and neighbors came to visit Dahlmann until his doctor decided to hospitalize Dahlmann. A hackney coach carried the weakened man to a hospital room where Dahlmann felt happy at the thought of sleeping in a room other than his own. Once in the hospital, however, he was subjected to bright lights, anesthetic, and an operation.

He awoke with the feeling of nausea, covered with a bandage, in a cell with something of a well about it; in the days and night which followed the operation he came to realize that he had merely been, up until then, in a suburb of hell. (136)

Dahlmann found that he hated himself and his ailing body but endured the painful cure until he broke under the stress of the news delivered by his physician: he had been close to death from septicemia. The news next related by the doctor brought Dahlmann round: he was healing well and would soon be able to leave for his ranch to recuperate.

It was autumn and as Dahlmann left the sanatorium he saw the changes of nature around him as a sign of his release from death. At the railroad station, he remembered that a cat lived in the café there. Dahlmann enjoyed the pleasures of finding the cat as he entered, stirring the sugar in his coffee and smoothing the cat's fur. Still, Dahlmann sensed that all these sensations were mere illusions. Once settled in the train, Dahlmann began to read from the first volume of *The Thousand and One Nights*, a book he fully associated with his fateful illness. The changing landscape outside his window, however, took his attention away from his book:

> *Tomorrow I'll wake up at the ranch*, he thought, and it was as if he was two men at a time: the man who traveled through the autumn day and across the geography of the fatherland, and the other one, locked up in a sanatorium. . . (138)

Dahlmann was caught up in thinking he recognized passing fields though in reality his was only a "nostalgic and literary knowledge" (138) of what he observed. Dahlmann came in and out of sleep and of dreams provoked by the movement of the train. Even the train seemed transfigured to Dahlmann.

Abruptly and unexpectedly, Dahlmann had to depart the train at an earlier stop. The attendant at this small station directed Dahlmann to the general store to arrange for a ride to his final destination. Rather than an inconvenience, Dahlmann accepted this change of events as a joyous adventure. He thought he recognized the store-owner, but realized the man might instead resemble an orderly from the hospital in Buenos Aires. Once in the store, Dahlmann decided to stay and eat. Then an old man caught Dahlmann's attention:

> He was dark, dried up, diminutive, and seemed outside time, situated in eternity. Dahlmann noted with satisfaction the kerchief, the thick poncho, the long chiripá, and the colt boots, and told himself, as he recalled futile discussions with people from the Northern counties or from the province of Entre Ríos, that gauchos like this no longer existed outside the South. (140)

Dahlmann ate and savored the taste of the wine as he drank. Dahlmann also noticed three country ruffians at one of the tables: two farmhands and a man who had Chinese features. He suddenly felt something glance off his face and saw a breadcrumb spitball on the tablecloth. He decided to concentrate on his book when another spitball hit the table. Dahlmann heard the men laugh out loud. The owner, calling Dahlmann by his name, told him to ignore the rowdy men. The mention of his name, however, seemed to transform the initial irritation into a personal provocation. Dahlmann engaged them directly. The Chinese-looking man approached him and lashed out with drunken insults. He tossed a knife in the air and challenged Dahlmann to a fight. Trying to avoid a confrontation, the storeowner pointed out that Dahlmann was unarmed.

Out of nowhere, the old gaucho threw Dahlmann a dagger. The man who was both "summary and cipher of the South (his South)" (141) had committed Dahlmann to the fight. Instinctively he picked up the dagger, knowing at the same time that it offered him no real defense. "*They would not have allowed such things to happen to me in the sanatorium*, he thought." (141) Dahlmann felt no fear, though; as he stepped outside he thought that it would have been a liberation to die in a duel that first night in the sanatorium. The text remains unclear whether Dahlmann, as he grasped the knife, faced his death or his dream of it.

LIST OF CHARACTERS IN
"The South"

Johannes Dahlmann: The paternal grandfather of the protagonist, Dahlmann, a minister in the Evangelical Church, emigrates to Buenos Aires in 1871.

Francisco Flores: A soldier in the Second Line-Infantry Division who fought and died—speared by an Indian lance—on the frontier of Buenos Aires. He is the central character's maternal and preferred grandfather and former owner of the Flores family ranch in the South.

Juan Dahlmann: The protagonist is quietly but proudly bound to his Argentine identity. Dahlmann is secretary of a municipal library who reveres the family ranch and dreams of spending time there. He falls ill suddenly and suffers through a painful cure. While on route to the ranch with the intention of a peaceful convalescence, Dahlmann becomes otherwise detained and must forcibly confront the untamed elements he finds in the South.

Storekeeper: This unnamed man helps Dahlmann to arrange for a ride to his family's estate. His general store and inn provide Dahlmann with needed rest as well as unwanted provocation.

Country louts: Three rough and drunken men—two farm hands and one of Chinese descent—taunt and threaten Dahlmann in the general store where they coerce Dahlmann into a fight.

Old man: Apparently down and out, this man exhibits all the characteristics of a gaucho from the South by his clothing and speech. Unexpectedly he provides the unarmed Dahlmann with a knife.

CRITICAL VIEWS ON

"The South"

JORGE LUIS BORGES ON THE STORY

[A poet in his own right (*Algebra of Night: New & Selected Poems*, 1948-1998 [1999]), Willis Barnstone has published numerous critical studies on Spanish poets such as Vicente Aleixandre and Antonio Machado, as well as on poetry by women and from China, including the poetry of Mao Tse Tung. The interview at hand took place at Indiana University in March 1976. In this excerpt, Borges answers a question from the audience on the conception of "El sur" ("The South").]

AUDIENCE: Could you tell us about your story "El Sur," "The South," how you conceived it, how it came about?

BORGES: I had been reading Henry James. I was greatly struck, as you all have been, by that story "The Turn of the Screw," which admits of several interpretations. You might think of the apparitions as being fiends masquerading as ghosts, and you might think of the children as being fools, or as being victims or perhaps accomplices. Henry James has written several stories rolled into one. Then I thought I would do the same thing myself. I would try the same trick by writing three stories at a time. Then I wrote "El Sur." In "El Sur," you will find three stories. You have firstly that of parody. There is a man being killed by the thing he loves. That is the reverse of what Oscar Wilde said: "For each man kills the thing he loves." That would be one version. Another would be if you read the story as being realistic. Then you also might have the most interesting interpretation, which doesn't exclude the others: you might think of the second half of the story as being what the man was dreaming when he died under the knife in the hospital. Because, really, that man was hungering after an epic death. He was inclined to die in the sharpness of the blades with a knife in his hand. He was actually dying under the surgeon's knife. So all that was dreamt up by him. I have the feeling that that was the interpretation. Really I think that story is a good story technically, because I tell those three stories at once, at one time. And they don't intrude on each other. That's what makes it interesting. You might have at first a parable. A man is thirsting for the south and when he goes back to the south, the south kills him. There you have the parable. Then the realistic story of the man going insane and of being made to fight with a drunken murderer. Then the third, which is the best, I think, that the whole thing is a dream. So the story would be not the actual death of the man, but the one he dreamt of while he was dying.

—Willis Barnstone, *Borges at 80: Conversations*. (Bloomington: Indiana University Press, 1982): p. 95.

JAIME ALAZRAKI ON STRUCTURE AND AUTOBIOGRAPHY IN THE STORY

[Professor Jaime Alazraki of Columbia University has written numerous scholarly works on major Latin American writers throughout his distinguished career, including *La prosa narrativa de Jorge Luis Borges* (1968) and *Narrativa y crítica de nuestra América* (1978) and has edited several collections of critical essays on Borges and Cortázar. In this fundamental study of the Kabbalistic echoes in the works of Borges, Professor Alazraki focuses on the autobiographical nature of the story as an essential element of its structure.]

The autobiographical character of this story is obvious. Juan Dahlmann is a mask of Borges, of a Borges who chooses, like his ancestor Laprida, books, but who knows that the deep reality of his other lineage is pierced by violence—a violence he abhors and whose futility he has repeatedly underlined, but which he recognizes as "an apocryphal past, at the same time stoic and orgiastic, in which any Argentine has defied and fought to finally fall silently in an obscure knife-fight." There is a second factor of a psychological nature. Grandchild and great-grandchild of colonels, offspring of heroes of the wars of independence, Borges has expressed in several poems his admiration for those military ancestors who shaped Argentine history. Secluded in a humble library, Borges has given in, more than once, to a nostalgic fascination for that past he views as epic. In his *Autobiographical Essay* he has said: "On both sides of my family I have military forebears; this may count for my yearning after that epic destiny which my gods denied me, no doubt wisely." Borges returns to that epic universe of his ancestors seeking neither a futile violence that he condemns nor an empty bravery that he insistently calls "useless," but a virtue that our time, predominantly individualistic, has forgotten. It is no accident that Bernard Shaw was one of his favorite writers. In him, Borges finds an alternative of liberation to the anxiety of modern man, and through Shaw he defines the meaning of that virtue he admires in his ancestors:

> Bernard Shaw is an author to whom I keep returning. . . . He has epic significance, and is the only writer of our time who has imagined and presented heroes to his readers. On the whole, modern writers tend to reveal men's weaknesses, and seem to delight in their unhappiness; in Shaw's case, however, we have characters like Major Barbara or Caesar, who are heroic and whom one can admire. Contemporary literature since Dostoievski—and even earlier, since Byron—seems to delight in man's guilt and weaknesses. In Shaw's work the greatest human virtues are extolled. For example, that a man can forget his own fate, that a man may not value his own happiness, that he may say like our Almafuerte: "I am not interested in my own life," because he is interested in something beyond personal circumstances.

In his heroic forefathers, Borges seeks to rescue that virtue: an epic sense of life, values that transcend the narrow limits of our individual selves and propose a stoic dimension that liberates life from its existential bounds. To the values of the novel—centered in the destiny of the self—Borges opposes the axiology of the epic: acts of courage that prove that people are capable of transcending their own egos in defense of humanistic ideals and elevated tasks. Violence is thus understood as a cathartic agent. The destruction of a life is not a gratuitous act, nor a macho's boastful display of guts. A hero—reasons Borges—defends a cause (a virtue, a destiny, a duty) whose value far exceeds that of his own life. In the duel between Juan Dahlmann and the boisterous *compadrito* who forces him to fight, Dahlmann succumbs as victim of a violence he has not chosen and of which he does not feel part, but in the final analysis the decision to fight is Dahlmann's. When Dahlmann bends over to pick up the knife thrown to him by "the old ecstatic gaucho in whom *he* saw a cipher of the South," he understands that he will be able to defend his injured dignity with the only language his provoker knows: the knife. The *compadrito* fights motivated by laws of honor which Borges has unequivocally condemned as a form of barbarism. Dahlmann's motivation is quite different. Dahlmann defends a moral value—his injured dignity—with his life. From this act one must conclude that for Dahlmann—for that Dahlmann who is dreaming his death in an innocuous hospital bed where he indeed is dying of "physical miseries"—dignity is dearer than the life that holds it. Viewed from this set of values, it is understandable that Dahlmann chose to pick up the knife that "would justify his killing." Between his death and the loss of his honor, Dahlmann chooses death.

But this choice is framed within a dream. When he is about to die of septicemia, prostrate in a hospital bed, Dahlmann confesses to himself that "if he had been able to choose, *then*, or to dream his death, this would have been the death he would have chosen or dreamt." The adverb (*then*) is important on two accounts. First, because it points to the circumstances under which that violent death was chosen. Second, because it refers to a literary dream that restores an Argentine myth: "a lowly knife fight dreamed by Hernández in the 1860's." Dahlmann's dream represents, in a way, the dream of all Argentines. It is just an avatar of that fight in which "a gaucho lifts a black off his feet with his knife, throws him down like a sack of bones, sees him agonize and die, crouches down to clean his blade, unties his horse, and mounts slowly so he will not be thought to be running away." Hernández's dream—Borges adds—"returns infinitely." The whole of Argentine history is ciphered in that dream that time has turned into a "part of the memory of all." Before dying, Dahlmann returns to that dream he knows he is part of. He chooses the dream of his *criollo* lineage, but only when nearing death. Dahlmann's life, devoted to books, has been an effort to correct the violence of that lineage. But as an Argentine vulnerable to the "imperatives of courage and honor," Dahlmann is forced to return to that "dream" of one man which is part of the memory of all, he is compelled to go back to that myth that defines the essence of his violent condition.

—Jaime Alazraki, "Structure as meaning in 'The South'." *Borges and the Kabbalah: And Other Essays on His Fiction and Poetry*, (Cambridge: Cambridge University Press, 1988): pp. 67-9.

Ana María Barrenchea on Repetition in Texts

[Professor Emeritus of the University of Buenos Aires, Ana María Barrenchea is the author *of La expressión de la irrealidad en la obra de Jorge Luis Borges* (1957; English ed. *Borges the Labyrinthmaker* [1965]). Her point of departure in this essay is based on a quote from Borges's *Otras inquisiciones (Other Inquisitions)* where he speaks of a history founded on diverse intonations of a few metaphors. For her investigation, Barrenchea concentrates on language and a repetition of events. In this excerpt, she compares similar events—the appearance of an old man—that occur in "El sur" ("The South") and "El hombre en el umbral" ("The Man on the Threshold").]

[But] in many instances the repetition of certain events, whether inverted or not, is found in different texts and can only be perceived within the macrostructure of Borges's entire oeuvre by those familiar with his work. One example that comes to mind is the old man who witnesses the final judgment in "The Man on the Threshold" (*AOS*), a figure repeated in the old gaucho who hands the knife to Dahlmann, the protagonist of "The South" (*F*). In the first story Borges gives the following description of this character:

> At my feet, motionless as an object, an old, old man squatted on the threshold. I'll tell what he was like, for he is an essential part of the story. His many years had worn him down and polished him as smooth as water polishes a stone, or as the generations of men polish a sentence. . . . I felt, on speaking these words, the pointlessness of questioning this old man for whom the present was hardly more than a dim rumor. (AOS 131–132)

The description is repeated almost verbatim in "The South": "On the floor, and hanging on to the bar, squatted an old man, immobile as an object. His years had reduced and polished him as water does a stone or the generations of man do a sentence. He was dark, dried up, diminutive, and seemed outside time, situated in eternity" (*F* 172). What is modified is the locale—from a house in India (which, Borges confesses, is itself a transformation of "the sudden and recurring glimpse into a deep set of corridors and patios of a tenement house around the corner from Paraná Street, in Buenos Aires" [*AOS* 274]) to the Argentine pampa. What is also varied is the man's clothing—a ragged tunic and turban in the first case; a kerchief, poncho, *chiripá*, and colt boots in the second. (This gaucho dress is intentionally archaic or anachronistic, that is, *a-chronic*.) But what is invariable is the comparison to a stone or a sentence, a comparison coined by Borges to underline the man's legendary old age.

In the Indian setting, the old man, a symbol of the divinity or of destiny, is untouched by the vicissitudes of life. This changes when he is placed in a Latin American environment. He still views humanity *sub specie aeternitatis*, but he is now touched by something we find in many of Borges's texts: the sense that we have hidden destinies blind as the blood we inherit. To quote from "The South": "From a corner of the room, the old ecstatic gaucho—in whom Dahlmann saw a summary and cipher of the South (his South)—threw him a naked dagger, which landed at his feet. It was as if the South had resolved that Dahlmann should accept the duel" (*F* 174). And the resolution is—paradoxically—both blindly obeyed and freely elected.

> —Ana María Barrenchea, "On the Diverse (South American) Intonation of Some (Universal) Metaphors." *Borges and His Successors: The Borgesian Impact on Literature and the Arts.* ed. Edna Aizenberg. (Columbia: University of Missouri Press, 1990): pp. 20-1.

EVELYN FISHBURN AND PSICHE HUGHES: DEFINITION OF GAUCHO

> [One of the goals of the editors of this dictionary included providing factual information for the reader. This entry supplies essential linguistic and anthropological background information regarding the figure of the gaucho who plays such a pivotal role in Dahlmann's destiny.]

Gaucho
The name for horsemen of Spanish, Negro and/or Indian blood who lived in the River Plate provinces and were known for their poverty, bravery and love of freedom. Traditionally nomadic, the *gauchos* worked in open cattle-ranching, but with the advent of wire fencing in the nineteenth century their free-roaming life came to an end. Today the term has connotations both of extreme bravery and laziness; the *gaucho* has become a literary, almost a mythical, figure. The etymology of the word is uncertain, and its interpretation can be taken as a barometer of the political climate. According to one theory, the word was originally *guacho*, from the Mapuche *huacho*, meaning orphaned, destitute. More recent research maintains that it originated in the border area between Argentina, Uruguay and Brazil, and means a deserter and cattle thief; it is still pronounced '*gaúcho*' there, and may stem from the Guarani *caúcho*, meaning a drunkard.
Lab. 30 (6) *Ficc.* 18

—Evelyn Fishburn and Psiche Hughes, *A Dictionary of Borges*, (London: Duckworth, 1990): p. 94.

Didier T. Jaén on Time (Fiction/Loss) in the Story

[Combined with the narrative techniques of writers including Proust, Joyce, and Faulkner, it is Jaén's belief that Borges exhibits a correlation of these concepts of time and narrative techniques. In this excerpt, he focuses on the challenges Borges faces when dealing with the differences between 'clock time' and 'mind-time' as seen in examples from "El sur" ("The South").]

Discussion and treatment of time in Borges' essays and fiction focus on certain dilemmas posed by the contrast between the concept of time and the experience of time, and on the solutions proposed to resolve those dilemmas. Even in realistic fiction, the confrontation of "real" time with our ideas of time poses certain problems. Chronological or clock time, is not always the measure for mind-time or psychological time. Borges' stories, such as "The Secret

Miracle," touch on this but more typically center on the problem of the distinction between the two.

In one of Borges' most realistic stories, "The South," the main character, Dahlmann, suffers a series of experiences that pose this problem. As a result of an accident, he is taken to the hospital where he develops septicemia and becomes gravely ill, almost to the point of death. At some point, he recovers and travels to the South to visit an old family ranch, his main link with his romantic Argentinean ancestry of gauchos and the Pampas. (In this story, traveling to the Argentinean South would be the equivalent of traveling to the American West in a Western romance or film. There may even be a "Western" cinematographic antecedent for the main scene of this story, as I shall presently indicate.) Dahlmann's trip is interrupted by a series of events that put him face to face with the South of his romantic past. A slight change in train schedule leaves him in a strange town where he decides to eat at the local "almacén" (a combination of country store and bar). In the "almacén" some young gauchos are eating and drinking at one of the tables while an old gaucho squats on the floor, leaning against the bar, "immobile as an object. His years had reduced and polished him as water does a stone or the generations of men do a sentence. He was dark, dried up, diminutive, and seemed outside time, situated in eternity" (F 172). The young gauchos harass Dahlmann to the point where a duel is inevitable, but he is a city man and carries no weapon. At this point, the old gaucho, "in whom Dahlmann saw a summary and cipher of the South (his South)" (F 174), throws him a knife. Dahlmann picks up the knife and walks out into the plain to confront his perhaps inevitable but romantic death.

In the prologue to *Ficciones*, where the story appeared, Borges made the following enigmatic comment: "Of 'The South,' which is perhaps my best story, let it suffice for me to suggest that it can be read as a direct narrative of novelistic events, and also in another way" (F 105-4). This comment thus became an integral part of the meaning or effect of the story which, without it, would most likely be read as a realistic story narrated in chronological order. Later he was more explicit: "'The South' is really a story of wishful thinking . . . Actually there are several plots. One of them might be that the man died on the operating table, and that the whole thing was a dream of his, in which he was striving to get the death he wanted" (Giovanni, 1973, 50).

> —Didier T. Jaén, "The Loss of Time." *Borges Esoteric Library: Metaphysics to Metafiction*. (Lanham, Maryland: University Press of America, 1992): pp. 120-1.

JORGE LUIS BORGES ON THE STORY

> [Rodman recalls here his question to Borges about "El sur" ("The South") during one of several conversations that took place in Buenos Aires in 1969, 1970, and 1972. Rodman starts the interview on the story while riding the elevator with Borges and finishes the chat with him some days later.]

We went to pay a call on Borges's mother who lives nearby and who is astonishingly alert at ninety-three. She moves, in fact, more nimbly than her son. Borges's sister Norah, who paints, was leaving as we entered the eighth-floor apartment. Señora Borges told us that she was reading English again—"lest I forget." ("Mother often calls me a quadroon," Borges confided behind his hand, "for being a fourth part English.") He had always lived with his mother, until two years ago his marriage to a widowed boyhood sweetheart in her fifties surprised his friends.

I asked Borges on the way down in the crowded elevator if my favorite among his stories, "El Sur" ("The South"), was autobiographical. Did it reflect a physical accident that had turned him from poetry to prose? "Yes, yes! of course, and it is one of my favorites too, because it is on so many levels—the autobiographical, the man who kills the thing he loves, the—"

The elevator came to a jerking stop, and we were spilled out into the lobby without my finding out what the other levels were.(. . .)

"What were the other levels," I asked Borges, "on which that story was written—the levels you were starting to tell me about the other day?"

"Well," he said, "one is that it was all perhaps a dream. You remember there's a circumstance hinted at in the beginning—that the protagonist may have died under the surgeon's knife. Then, at the inn, the protagonist has the *Arabian Nights* with him again, and the storekeeper is like the intern at the hospital, and the store reminds him of an engraving. So couldn't it all be a dream at the moment of dying? . . . The autobiographical level is in the thinking of the violent death of his grandfather—as I did so often of mine. A student once asked me in Texas: 'When did the protagonist die?' I answered: 'You pays your money and you takes your choice!...' Still another level is the protagonist's love for the South—and its symbolic knife. He loves it, and it kills him."

I thought of the exaltation of courage in Borges's poems, not the physical courage he may have lacked, or thought he lacked as a young man—as some have conjectured—but courage as a spiritual legacy, as in the poem about his great-grandfather, who turned the tide during the Battle of Junín:

> ...His great-grandson is writing these lines,
> and a silent voice comes to him out of the past,
> out of the blood:
>
> "What does my battle at Junín matter if it is only
> a glorious memory, or a date learned by rote
> for an examination, or a place in the atlas?
> The battle is everlasting and can do without
> the pomp of actual armies and of trumpets.
> Junín is two civilians cursing a tyrant
> on a street corner,
> or an unknown man somewhere dying in prison."

"A Page to Commemorate Colonel Suárez,
Victor at Junín," *Selected Poems 1923–1967*

>—Selden Rodman, "Jorge Luis Borges." *Jorge Luis Borges: Conversations*, ed. Richard Burgin (Jackson: University Press of Mississippi, 1998): pp. 95 and 105-6.

WORKS BY
Jorge Luis Borges

Fervor de Buenos Aires. 1923.
Inquisiciones. 1925.
Luna de enfrente. 1925.
El tamaño de mi esperanza. 1926.
El idioma de los argentinos. 1928.
Cuaderno San Martín. 1929.
Evaristo Carriego. 1930.
Discussión. 1932.
Historia universal de la infamia. 1935.
Historia de la eternidad. 1936.
El jardín de los senderos que se bifurcan. 1941.
Ficciones (1935-1944). 1944.
Nueva refutación del tiempo. 1947.
El Aleph. 1949.
Otras inquisiciones (1937-1952). 1952.
El hacedor. 1960.
Antología personal. 1961.
Obra poética (1923-1964). 1964.
Para las seis cuerdas. 1965.
Nueva antología personal. 1968.
Elogio de la sombra. 1969.
El otro, el mismo. 1969.
El informe de Brodie. 1970.
El libro de arena. 1975.
La rosa profunda. 1975.
La moneda de hierro. 1976.
Historia de la noche. 1977.
Obras completas en colaboración. 1979.

Obra poética: 1923-1976. 1979.
La cifra. 1981.
Nueve ensayos dantescos. 1982.
Vienticinco agosto 1983 y otros cuentos. 1983.
Los conjurados. 1985.

PRINCIPAL TRANSLATIONS IN ENGLISH

Ficciones. trans. Anthony Kerrigan and others. 1962.

Labyrinths: Selected Stories and Other Writings. ed. Donald A. Yates and James E. Irby. 1962.

Dreamtigers. (El hacedor). trans. Mildred Boyer and Harold Morland. 1964.

Other Inquisitions 1937-1952. trans. Ruth L. C. Simms. 1964.

A Personal Anthology. ed. Anthony Kerrigan. 1967.

The Aleph and Other Stories: 1933-1969. ed. and trans. Norman Thomas di Giovanni in collaboration with the author. 1970.

Doctor Brodie's Report. trans. Norman Thomas di Giovanni in collaboration with the author. 1972.

Selected Poems 1923-1967. trans. Norman Thomas di Giovanni and others. 1972.

A Universal History of Infamy. trans. Norman Thomas di Giovanni. 1972.

In Praise of Darkness. trans. Norman Thomas di Giovanni. 1974.

The Book of Sand. trans. Norman Thomas di Giovanni. 1977.

The Gold of the Tigers: Selected Later Poems. trans. Alastair Reid. 1977.

Evaristo Carriego: A Book about Old-Time Buenos Aires. trans. NormanThomas di Giovanni. 1983.

Atlas. trans. Anthony Kerrigan. 1985.

Ficciones. intro. John Sturrock. 1993.

Collected Fictions. trans. Andrew Hurley. 1998.

Selected Non-Fiction. Eliot Weinberger, ed. New York: Penguin, 1999.

WORKS ABOUT
Jorge Luis Borges

Aizenberg, Edna. *The Aleph Weaver: Biblical, Kabbalistic and Judaic Elements in Borges.* Potomac, Maryland: Scripta Humanistica, 1984.

Alazraki, Jaime. *La prosa narrativa de Jorge Luis Borges.* Madrid: Gredos, 1968.

———, ed. *Jorge Luis Borges.* Madrid: Taurus, 1976.

———. *Borges and the Kabbalah: And Other Essays on His Fiction and Poetry.* Cambridge: Cambridge University Press, 1988.

Balderston, Daniel. *The Literary Universe of Jorge Luis Borges: An Index to References and Allusions to Persons, Titles, and Places in His Writings.* Westport, CT: Greenwood Press, 1986.

Barnstone, Willis. *Borges at Eighty: Conversations.* Bloomington: Indiana University Press, 1982.

Barrenechea, Ana Maria. *La expresión de la irrealidad en la obra de Jorge Luis Borges.* Mexico City: El Colegio de Mexico, 1957.

———. *Borges the Labyrinth Maker.* trans. Robert Lima. New York: New York University Press, 1965.

———. "On the Diverse (South American) Intonation of Some (Universal) Metaphors," *Borges and His Successors: The Borgesian Impact on Literature and the Arts.* ed. Edna Aizenberg. Columbia: University of Missouri Press, 1990:17-25.

Bloom, Harold, ed. *Modern Critical Views: Jorge Luis Borges.* Philadelphia: Chelsea House, 1986.

———. *The Western Canon: The Books and School of the Ages.* New York: Harcourt Brace & Company, 1994.

Borges, Jorge Luis. *The Aleph and Other Stories: 1933-1969.* ed. and trans. Norman Thomas di Giovanni. New York: E. P. Dutton Co., Inc., 1970.

———. *Ficciones.* intro. John Sturrock. New York: Knopf, 1993.

———. *Collected Fictions.* trans. Andrew Hurley. New York: Penguin, 1998.

Burgin, Richard. *Conversations with Jorge Luis Borges.* New York: Holt, Rinehart and Winston, 1969.

———. ed. *Jorge Luis Borges: Conversations*. Jackson: University Press of Mississippi, 1998.

Carter, Angela."Borges the Taxonomist" in *The Borges Tradition*. ed. Norman Thomas di Giovanni. (London: Constable, 1995): 35-47.

Christ, Ronald J. "The Art of Fiction: Jorge Luis Borges.' *Paris Review 40* (1967): 116-64.

———. *The Narrow Act: Borges' Art of Allusion*. New York: New York University Press, 1969.

———. 'Forking Narratives," *Simply a Man of Letters,* ed. Carlos Cortínez. Orono: University of Maine Press, 1982: 75-88.

de Costa, René. *Humor in Borges*. Detroit: Wayne State University Press, 2000.

di Giovanni, Norman Thomas, and others. *Borges on Writing*. New York: Dutton, 1973.

Donoso, José. *The Boom in Spanish American Literature: A Personal History*. trans. G. Kolovakos. New York: Columbia University Press, 1977.

Dunham, Lowell, and Ivar Ivask, ed. *The Cardinal Points of Borges*. Norman: University of Oklahoma Press, 1971.

Elia, Nada. "Islamic Esoteric Concepts as Borges Strategies." *Variaciones Borges* 5 (1998): 129-44.

Evans, Michael. "Intertextual Labyrinth: 'El inmortal' by Borges." *Forum for Modern Language Studies*. 20 (July 1984): 275-81.

Fishburn, Evelyn and Psiche Hughes. *A Dictionary of Borges*. London: Duckworth, 1990.

Fló, Juan, ed. *Contra Borges*. Buenos Aires: Galerna, 1978.

Foster, David William. *Studies in the Contemporary Spanish American Short Story*. Columbia: University of Missouri Press, 1979.

———. *Jorge Luis Borges: An Annotated Primary and Secondary Bibliography*. New York and London: Garland, 1984.

Fuentes, Carlos. "The Accidents of Time" in *The Borges Tradition*. ed. Norman Thomas di Giovanni. London: Constable, 1995 : 49-69.

González-Casanovas, Roberto J. "Borges' Argentinian South: Legend, Fiction, and Myth in 'El sur'." *Philological Papers*. 37

(1991): 151-7.

González Echevarría, Roberto. *Myth and Archive: A Theory of Latin American narrative*. Cambridge: Cambridge University Press, 1990.

———, ed. *The Oxford Book of Latin American Short Stories*. New York: Oxford University Press, 1997.

Gonzalez Echevarria, Roberto and Enrique Pupo-Walker. *The Cambridge History of Latin American Literature*. 3 vols. Cambridge: Cambridge University Press, 1995.

Hernández Martín, Jorge. *Readers and Labyrinths*. New York: Garland, 1995.

Jaén, Didier T. "The Esoteric Tradition in Borges' 'Tlön, Uqbar, Orbis Tertius'.".*Studies in Short Fiction* 21 (Winter 1984): 25-39.

———. *Borges' Esoteric Library: Metaphysics to Metafiction*. Lanham, Maryland: University Press of America, 1992.

Jitrik, Noé. "Estructura y significación en *Ficciones* de Jorge Luis Borges." *Casa de las Americas* 53 (1969) :50-62.

Josipovici, Gabriel. "Borges and the Plain Sense of Things" in *Borges and Euorpe Revisited*. ed. Evelyn Fishburn. (London: University of London, 1998): 60-7.

Jullien, Dominique. "Biography of an Immortal." *Comparative Literature* 47 (Spring 1995): 136-59.

Kodama de Borges, María. "Jorge Luis Borges, Religions and the Mystical Experience" in *Jorge Luis Borges: Thought and Knowledge in the XXth Century*. eds. Alfonso de Toro and Fernando de Toro. Frankfurt: Vervuert, 1999: 15-27.

Lindstrom, Naomi. *Jorge Luis Borges: A Study of the Short Fiction*. Boston: Twayne Publishers, 1990.

McMurray, George R. *Jorge Luis Borges*. New York: Frederick Ungar Publishing Co., 1980.

Menocal, María Rosa. *Writing in Dante's Cult of Truth: From Borges to Boccaccio*. Durham: Duke University Press, 1991.

Merrell, Floyd. *Unthinking Thinking: Jorge Luis Borges, Mathematics, and the New Physics*. West Laffayette, Indiana: Purdue University Press, 1991.

———. "Borges and Calvino: Chaosmos Unleashed," *Jorge Luis Borges: Thought and Knowledge in the XXth Century*. eds.

Alfonso de Toro and Fernando de Toro. Frankfurt: Vervuert, 1999. pp. 175-205.

Molloy, Silvia. *La diffusion de la littérature hispano-américaine en France au XX siécle.* Paris: Presses Universitaires de France, 1972.

———. *Signs of Borges.* Durham: Duke University Press, 1994.

Østergård, Svend. "The Unconscious of Representation." *Variaciones Borges* 1 (1996): 101-12.

Rodman, Selden. *Tongues of Fallen Angels; Conversations with Jorge Luis Borges.* New York, New Directions Publishing, 1974.

Rodriguez Monegal, Emir. *Jorge Luis Borges: A Literary Biography.* New York: Dutton, 1978.

Sorrentino, Fernando. *Siete conversaciones con Jorge Luis Borges.* Buenos Aires: Casa Pardo, 1973.

Stewart, Jon. "Borges on Immortality." *Philosophy and Literature.* 17 (October 1993): 295-301.

Sturrock, John. *Paper Tigers: The Ideal Fictions of Jorge Luis Borges.* Oxford: Clarendon, 1977.

Thiem, Jon. "Borges, Dante, and the Poetics of Total Vision." *Comparative Literature.* 40 (Spring 1988): 97-121.

Updike, John. 'Books: The Author as Librarian.' *New Yorker,* 30 October 1965, 223-46.

Urraca, Beatriz. "Wor(l)ds Through the Looking-Glass: Borges's Mirrors and Contemporary Theory." *Revista Canadiense de Estudios Hispánicos.* 17 (Otoño 1992) : 153-76.

Wheelock, Carter. *The Mythmaker: A Study of Motif and Symbol in the Short Stories* of *Jorge Luis Borges.* Austin: University of Texas Press, 1969.

ACKNOWLEDGMENTS

"Commentaries", from *THE ALEPH AND OTHER STORIES* by Jorge Luis Borges, translated by Norman Thomas di Giovanni, copyright © 1968, 1969, 1970 by Emece Editores, S.A. and Norman Thomas di Giovanni. Used by permission of Dutton, a division of Penguin Putnam Inc.

"The Diverse Intonation of Some Jewish Metaphors" by Edna Aizenberg from *The Aleph Weaver: Biblical, Kabbalistic and Judaic Elements in Borges* © 1984 by Scripta Humanistica. Reprinted by Permission.

A Dictionary of Borges by Evelyn Fishburn and Psiche Hughes © 1990 by Gerald Duckworth and Company.

"Borges, Neruda, and Pessoa: Hispanic-Portugues Whitman" by Harold Bloom from *The Western Canon: The Books and School of the Ages* © 1994 by Harcourt Brace & Company. Reprinted by Permission.

"The Accidents of Time" by Carlos Fuentes from *The Borges Tradition*, ed. Norman Thomas di Giovanni © 1995 by Constable. Reprinted by Permission.

"'Death and the Compass': Lönnrot's Last Case?" by Jorge Hernández Martín from *Readers and Labyrinths* © 1995 by Garland. Reprinted by Permission.

"The Unconscious of Representation" by Svend Østergård from *Variaciones Borges* 1 © 1996 by *Variaciones Borges*. Reprinted by Permission.

"Borges and Calvino: Chaosmos Unleashed" by Floyd Merrell from *Jorge Luis Borges: Thought and Knowledge in the XXth Century*, eds. Alfonso de Toro and Fernando de Toro © 1999 by Vervuert. Reprinted by Permission.

"The Esoteric Tradition in Borges' 'Tlon, Uqbar, Orbis Tertius'" by Didier T. Jaén from *Studies in Short Fiction* 21 © 1984 by *Studies in Short Fiction*. Reprinted by Permission.

"The Novel as Myth and Archive: Ruins and Relics of Tlön" by Roberto González Echevarría from *Myth and Archive: A Theory of Latin American Narrative* © 1990 by Cambridge University Press. Reprinted with the permission of Cambridge University Press.

"Wor(l)ds Through the Looking-Glass: Borges's Mirrors and Contemporary Theory" by Beatriz Urraca from *Revista Canadiense de Estudios Hispánicos* 17 © 1992 by Beatriz Urraca. Reprinted by Permission.

"Converting the Simulacrum," ed., Sylvia Molloy from *Signs of Borges*, trans. Oscar Montero. Copyright © 1994, Duke University Press. All rights reserved. Reprinted with Permission.

"Borges and the Plain Sense of Things" by Gabriel Josipovici from *Borges and Europe Revisited*. ed. Evelyn Fishburn © 1998 by University of London. Reprinted by Permission.

Jorge Luis Borges: Conversations, ed. Richard Burgin © 1998 by University Press of Mississippi. Reprinted by Permission.

"Borges and the Absurd Human Condition" by George R. McMurray from *Jorge Luis Borges* © 1980 by The Continuum Publishing Company. Reprinted by permission of the Continuum International Publishing Group.

"Intertextual Labyrinth: 'El inmortal' by Borges" by Michael Evans from *Forum for Modern Language Studies* 20 © 1984 by Oxford University Press. Reprinted by Permission.

Stewart, Jon. "Borges on Immortality." *Philosophy and Literature* 17:2 (1993), 300-301.© The Johns Hopkins University Press. Reprinted by permission of the Johns Hopkins University Press.

"Biography of an Immortal" by Dominique Julien from *Comparative Literature* Vol. 47 © 1995 by *Comparative Literature*. Reprinted by Permission.

"Fun in *Fictions* and *The Aleph*" by René de Costa from *Humor in Borges* © 2000 by Wayne State University Press. Reprinted by Permission.

"Borges, Dante, and the Poetics of Total Vision" by Jon Thiem from *Comparative Literature* 40 © 1988 by *Comparative Literature*. Reprinted by Permission.

"Blindness, Alephs and Lovers" by María Rosa Menocal from *Writing in Dante's Cult of Truth: From Borges to Boccaccio* © 1991 by Duke University Press. Reprinted by Permission.

"Islamic Esoteric Concepts as Borges Strategies" by Nada Elia from *Variaciones Borges* 5 © 1998 by *Variaciones Borges*. Reprinted by Permission.

"Jorges Luis Borges, Religions and the Mystical Experience" by María Kodama de Borges from *Jorge Luis Borges: Thought and Knowledge in the XXth Century*. Eds. Alfonso de Toro and Fernando de Toro © 1999 by Vervuert. Reprinted by Permission.

Borges at 80: Conversations, Willis Barnstone, ed. © 1982 by Indiana University Press. Reprinted by Permission.

"Structure as meaning in 'The South'" by Jaime Alazraki from *Borges and the Kabbalah: And Other Essays on His Fiction and Poetry* © 1988 by Cambridge University Press. Reprinted with permission of Cambridge University Press.

"On the Diverse (South American) Intonation of Some (Universal) Metaphors" by Ana Maria Barrenchea. Reprinted from *Borges and His Successors: The Borgesian Impact on Literature and the Arts* by Edna Aizenberg, by permission of the University of Missouri Press. Copyright © 1990 by the Curators of the University of Missouri.

"The Loss of Time" by Didier T. Jaén from *Borges Esoteric Library: Metaphysics to Metafiction* © 1992 by the University Press of America. Reprinted by Permission.

Dembo, L.S. "An Interview with Jorge Luis Borges." Contemporary Literature, Vol. 11, No. 3. © 1970. Reprinted by permission of The University of Wisconsin Press.

INDEX OF
Themes and Ideas

"ALEPH, THE"; 79-95; Beatriz in, 79-81, 89, and visions of, 87-90; beloved in, 88; Borges in, 79-81, 88-89; Borges view of story, 84-85; character list, 82-83; critical view, 84-95; Daneri in 79-81, 88-89, and his *The Earth*, 79, and his link to Aleph, 88-89; and Dante's *Paradiso*, 85-86; definition of Aleph, 86-87; Islamic mysticism in, 91-93; mystical experiences in, 93-95; the narrator in, 79-81, and his desperation, 94-95; parallels to Dante, 85-86; plot summary, 79-81; rivalry in, 92-93; the story, 90-91; total vision and verbal art in, 86; and "Zahin, The," 92

BORGES, JORGE LUIS: on "Aleph, The," 90-91; biography of, 12-15; on death, 30; on "Death and the Compass", 23-24; humor of, 76-78; interview with, 60-61; on James, Henry, 100-101; parallels with Dante, 85-86; connection to Buenos Aires, 30-31; on "South, The", 100-101, 108-109; on Wilde, Oscar, 100-101

"DEATH AND THE COMPASS", 16-39; aesthetic motivations of, 28-29; azevedo, 18-20; character list, 21-22; the city and fiction, 29-31, 33; critical views, 23-39; cryptic message, 16; detective fiction, 31-33; game in, 31-34; Ginsberg in, 17, 20; human struggle to comprehend universe, 25-27; inspector Treviranus in, 17-19, 34-37; Jew-as-mind in, 26-27; Jewish elements and Spinoza, 24-28; *Judische Zeitung*, 16; Kabbalah in, 24; labyrinths and the story, 35-39; literary mode, 24, 28-29; Lonnot in, 17-19; 34-37, and as pure reasoner in, 25, and scheme of , 37, and Spinoza, 26-27; murder in, 16-17; 25-26, 33-34; plot summary, 16-20; and "Purloined Letter, The," 31-32; Rabbi Marcel in, 16; representation in, 33-35; Scharlach in, 18-20, 34, 39; Spinoza theory, 26; the story, 23-24; time and space patterns in, 23-24

FEVOR DE BUENOS AIRES, 30

"IMMORTAL, THE," 62-78; an allegory of creative process, 67-68; Argos in, 64-65 and Homer, 69; biographies of an immortal, 74-76; character list, 66; Christian view of immortality in, 71-73; communication in, 64; critical views, 67-78; definition of Argos, 70-71; definition of Cartaphilis, Joseph, 70; epithet, 62; and

Homer, 68-70; humor in, 76-78; intertextuality in, 68-70; irony in, 73-74; literary idealism in, 73-74; 'mad' city, 67; Marcus in, 63-67; narrator on the found manuscript, 62-65; problem of representation, 72; the protagonist, 75-76; wandering Jew in, 75-76

"SOUTH, THE", 96-109; and *Arabian Nights*, 109; Argentine history in, 101-102; as autobiographical 101-104, 108-109; character list, 99; choice of violence in, 102-103; critical views, 100-109; epic sense of life in, 102; definition of Gaucho, 105-106; dilemmas in, 106-107; and "El Sur," 108; and *Ficciones*, 107; fiction and loss in, 106-108; Johannes in, 96-98; Juan in, 96-98; and as autobiographical, 101-102, and death of, 102-103, 107; plot summary, 96-98; repeated locale in, 105; repetition of text, 104-105; and "Secret Miracle, The," 107; several plots of, 107-108; the story by Borges, 100-101, 108-109

"TLÖN, UQBAR, ORBIS TERTIUS," 40-61; artifice of regionalist novel, 50; Bioy in, 40-44; Borges in, 40-44; character list, 45-46; critical views, 47-61; definition of Orbis Tertius, 49-50; esoteric tradition, 47-49; and Frazer's "The Golden Bough," 51; ideologies in, 57-60; interview in 60-61; language in, 55-57; as limp critique of times, 59; literature of Uqbar, 42-44, and its connection to Tlön, 47-48; mirror in, 40, and Tlön, 60-61; narrator in, 41-44, 58-59; plot summary, 40-44; poetic objects in, 56-58; political aspects in, 59-60; point of story, 58-59; proposed encyclopedia in, 47, 49, 52-54; and reflections of, 54; the story, 50-53, 58; Tlön, 42-61